# e.explore

# Human Body

LONDON, NEW YORK, MELBOURNE,
MUNICH and DELHI

**Project Editors** Dr Rob Houston, Esther Ripley
**Editors** Rosie O'Neill, Kitty Blount, Andrea Mills

**Weblink Editors** Niki Foreman, Phil Hunt, Clare Lister

**Managing Editor** Linda Esposito

**Digital Development Manager** Fergus Day
**DTP Co-ordinator** Tony Cutting

**Jacket Copywriter** Adam Powley
**Jacket Editor** Mariza O'Keeffe

**Publishing Managers** Andrew Macintyre, Caroline Buckingham

**Consultant** Dr Sue Davidson

**Senior Designers** Owen Peyton Jones, Jacqui Swan, Adrienne Hutchinson

**Illustrators** Robin Hunter, Lee Gibbons, Rajeev Doshi

**Managing Art Editor** Diane Thistlethwaite

**Picture Researchers** Franziska Marking, Marie Ortu
**Picture Librarians** Sarah Mills, Kate Ledwith

**Production** Emma Hughes
**Jacket Designer** Neal Cobourne

**Art Director** Simon Webb

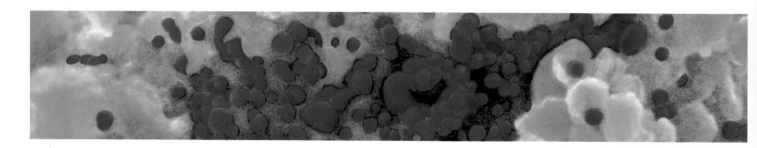

First published in Great Britain in 2005
by Dorling Kindersley Limited, 80 Strand, London WC2R 0RL

Penguin Group

Copyright © 2005 Dorling Kindersley Limited

Google™ is a trademark of Google Technology Inc.

2 4 6 8 10 9 7 5 3 1

A CIP catalogue for this book is available from the British Library.

ISBN 1 4053 0364 6

Colour reproduction by Colourscan, Singapore
Printed in China by Toppan Printing Co. (Shenzen) Ltd.

Discover more at
**www.dk.com**

# e.explore

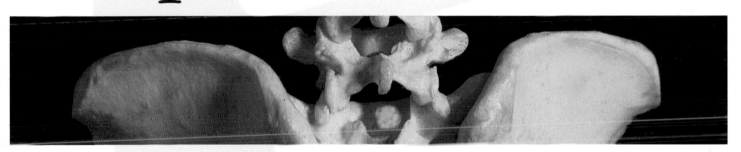

# Human Body

Written by **Richard Walker**

Google

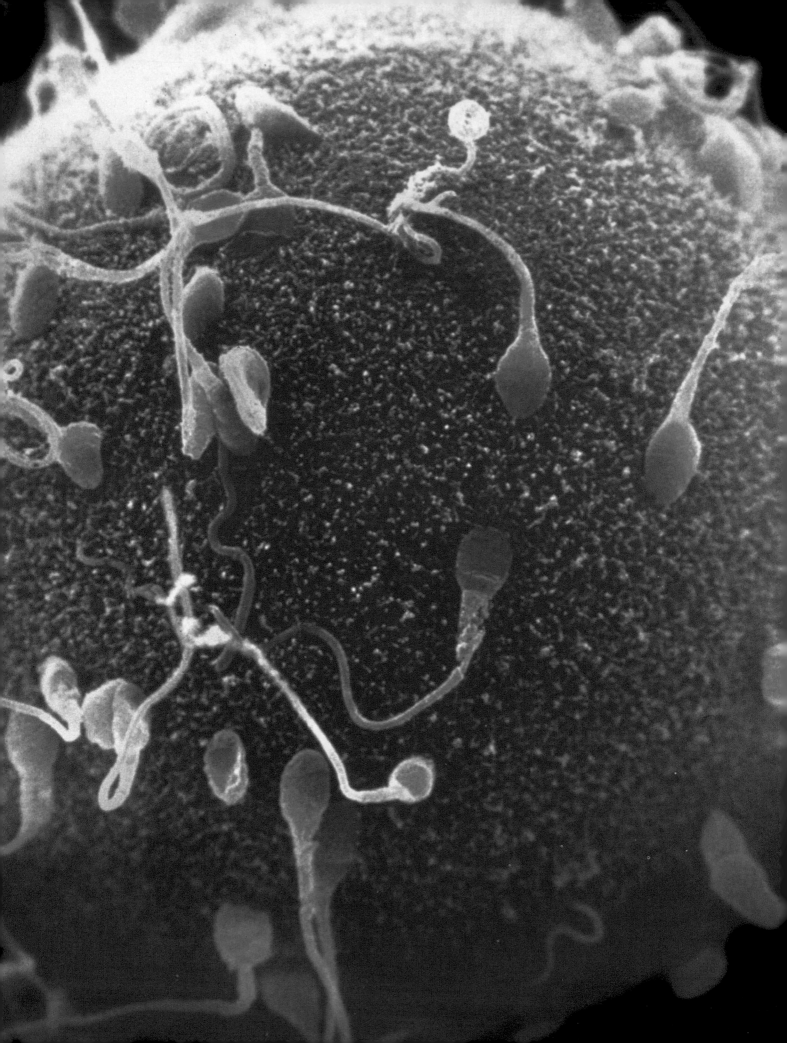

# CONTENTS

# How to use the e.explore website

e.explore Human Body has its own website, created by DK and Google™. When you look up a subject in the book, the article gives you key facts and displays a keyword that links you to extra information online. Just follow these easy steps.

# http://www.humanbody.dke-explore.com

**1**    Enter this website address...

Address :   http://www.humanbody.dke-explore.com

**2**    Find the keyword in the book...

vision

**3**    Enter the keyword...

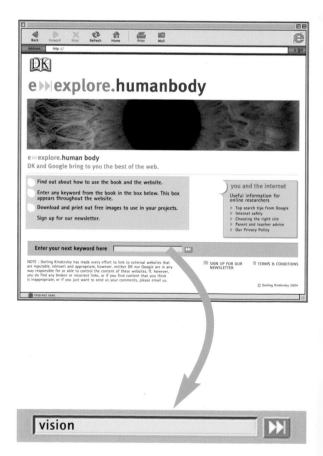

vision

You can use only the keywords from the book to search on our website for the specially selected DK/Google links.

## Be safe while you are online:

- Always get permission from an adult before connecting to the internet.

- Never give out personal information about yourself.

- Never arrange to meet someone you have talked to online.

- If a site asks you to log in with your name or email address, ask permission from an adult first.

- Do not reply to emails from strangers – tell an adult.

**Parents:** Dorling Kindersley actively and regularly reviews and updates the links. However, content may change. Dorling Kindersley is not responsible for any site but its own. We recommend that children are supervised while online, that they do not use Chat Rooms, and that filtering software is used to block unsuitable material.

**4** Click on your chosen link...

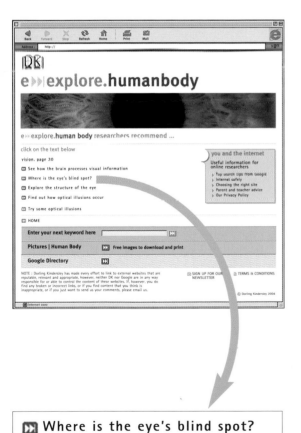

▶▶ Where is the eye's blind spot?

Links include animations, videos, sound buttons, virtual tours, interactive quizzes, databases, timelines, and realtime reports.

**5** Download fantastic pictures...

Pictures | Human Body ▶▶

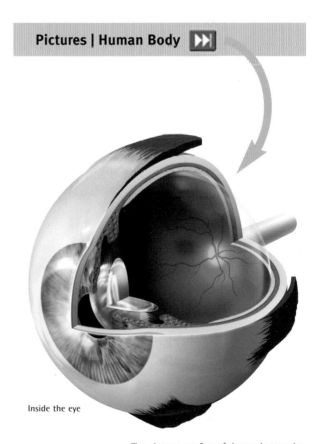

Inside the eye

The pictures are free of charge, but can be used for personal non-commercial use only.

## Go back to the book for your next subject...

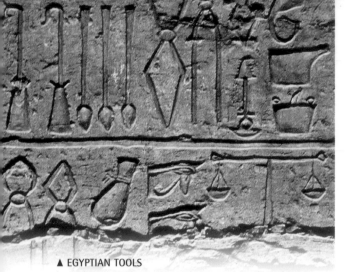

**▲ EGYPTIAN TOOLS**
In ancient times, humans were just as curious about the human body, and why it goes wrong, as we are today. Egypt boasted some of the greatest physicians of the ancient world, who dissected bodies to discover more about their workings, performed simple surgery, and also recorded their findings. More than 2,000 years old, this bas-relief from a temple north of Aswan, Egypt, shows some of the surgical instruments used by early doctors.

# EXPLORING THE BODY

Our understanding of the human body is the result of centuries of exploration. In Europe, major advances were made after the 16th century when the dissection of bodies was permitted. With the use of the first anaesthetics in the 19th century, surgery became more complex, and the discovery of X-rays supplied the first method of seeing inside the body without cutting it open. Since the second half of the 20th century, more sophisticated imaging techniques have enabled doctors and scientists to watch the living body in action and to diagnose disease more easily.

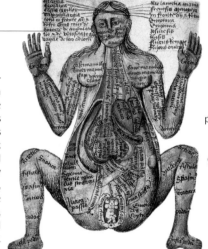

*Drawing of a woman accompanied by astrological text*

**MYTH NOT REALITY ▶**
Until the Renaissance of the 15th and 16th centuries, knowledge about the human body was dominated by the teachings of 2nd-century Greek physician Galen. His beliefs and misconceptions about the body went unchallenged. Drawings, such as this one of female anatomy from the 15th century, were flat and inaccurate and owed more to myth than reality.

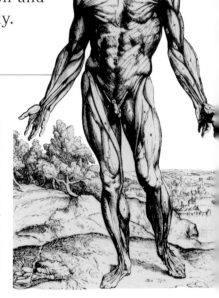

*Arm muscles drawn in accurate detail*

**ANATOMICAL ACCURACY ▶**
Previously banned in Europe, the dissection of bodies was finally permitted in the 16th century. Flemish doctor Andreas Vesalius carried out dissections and, with the help of a gifted artist, published his findings in his book *On the Structure of the Human Body* in 1543. His accurate descriptions of anatomy, such as this one of skeletal muscles, challenged previous wisdom and advanced understanding of the human body.

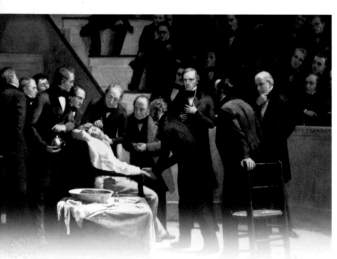

**▲ ANAESTHETICS**
Using an anaesthetic allows surgeons to perform surgery without the patient feeling pain. An anaesthetic (ether) was first used in Boston in 1846 during surgery to remove a neck tumour (above). Before this, surgery had to be done as fast as possible because it caused terrible pain. Anaesthetics allowed doctors to attempt more complex surgery and to discover far more about the living body.

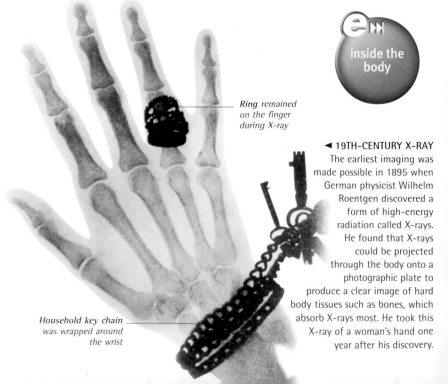

*Ring remained on the finger during X-ray*

**e ▸▸
inside the body**

**◀ 19TH-CENTURY X-RAY**
The earliest imaging was made possible in 1895 when German physicist Wilhelm Roentgen discovered a form of high-energy radiation called X-rays. He found that X-rays could be projected through the body onto a photographic plate to produce a clear image of hard body tissues such as bones, which absorb X-rays most. He took this X-ray of a woman's hand one year after his discovery.

*Household key chain was wrapped around the wrist*

*Section through brain clearly shows its parts*

*Bladder filled with urine*

*Calf muscle*

## PRESENT-DAY IMAGING

### PET SCAN
Positron emission tomography (PET) scanning is used to show how active a tissue is. This PET scan shows activity (coloured patches) in the left side of the brain when a person is speaking. The person was given radioactive glucose, which was taken up by active brain cells. These give off radioactive positrons, which are detected by a PET scanner.

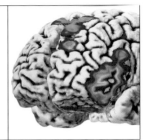

### CT SCAN
Computed tomography (CT) scanning uses a scanner that rotates around the body sending X-rays. These pass through body tissues into a detector linked to a computer, which produces images in the form of "slices" through the body. These can be built into 3-D images like this one of the ribcage, shoulders, and backbone.

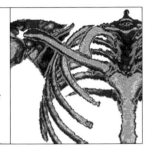

### ULTRASOUND
During ultrasound scanning, pulses of high frequency sound are beamed into the body. When reflected by tissues, these sound waves create echoes, which are converted into computer images. Ultrasound scans are a safe way to monitor a fetus (right) inside the uterus. They also show movement, such as the beating of the heart.

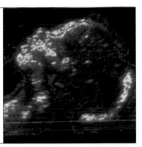

### CONTRAST RADIOGRAPHY
Conventional X-rays provide clear images of hard structures in the body, such as bones, but not soft tissues. Contrast radiography uses a substance that absorbs X-rays to highlight soft, hollow organs. Here barium sulphate has been introduced into the large intestine to show its structure. The image has been coloured artificially.

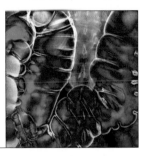

### MRA
Magnetic resonance angiography (MRA) is a form of MRI (left) that is used to provide clear images of blood vessels. A substance is sometimes injected before the scan to make blood vessels easier to see. This scan shows healthy arteries (red) in the lower abdomen with the aorta (top) dividing into left and right common iliac arteries.

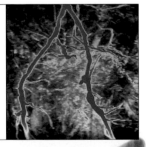

### SEM
Although not an imaging technique as such, scanning electron microscopy produces images of dead cells and body tissues. The microscope scans an object with a beam of electrons to produce a 3-D image. This is photographed and saved as a scanning electron micrograph (SEM). This SEM shows a hair (green) emerging from the skin (pink).

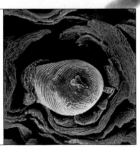

*Nanorobot locks onto and kills bacterium*

*Disease-causing bacterium is inside the body*

### ▲ MRI SCAN
Magnetic resonance imaging (MRI) is a modern imaging technique that produces high-definition images of soft tissues, such as the brain. During MRI scanning, a patient lies inside a tunnel-like scanner and is exposed painlessly to a powerful magnetic field and to bursts of radio waves. These cause molecules in the body to release energy. When analyzed by a computer, this produces images, like this vertical section through a woman.

### ▲ NANOTECHNOLOGY
One day it may be possible to use tiny robots, called nanorobots, to patrol the human body. Built using advanced nanotechnology and powered by energy from glucose and oxygen in the blood, minuscule nanorobots, such as those illustrated above, could aid the body's defences by finding and disabling disease-causing bacteria. Other possible uses include repairing damaged blood vessels.

# BUILDING BLOCKS

Some 100 trillion (100,000,000,000,000) microscopic living units called cells are the body's building blocks. We know what cells look like and how they work through the use of light microscopes and, more recently, powerful electron microscopes. There are around 200 different types of cell in the body, including the epithelial, adipose, nerve, egg, and sperm cells described here. Cells differ in shape, size, and function, but all share certain characteristics. Each has a cell membrane, a nucleus, and jelly-like cytoplasm containing organelles, which perform a variety of functions that support the cell. Cell division allows the body to make new cells to replace those lost by damage and wear, and to enable young bodies to grow.

▲ CHEEK CELLS UNDER A LIGHT MICROSCOPE
Just as paving slabs cover a path, so these broad, squarish, epithelial cells cover the inner lining of the cheeks. This image was obtained using a light microscope. It shows the nucleus (orange) and cytoplasm (green) of each cell, however the magnification is not sufficient to reveal the structures suspended in the cytoplasm that are shown in the model below. Cheek cells belong to a group of cells called epithelial cells that cover and line the body's inner and outer surfaces.

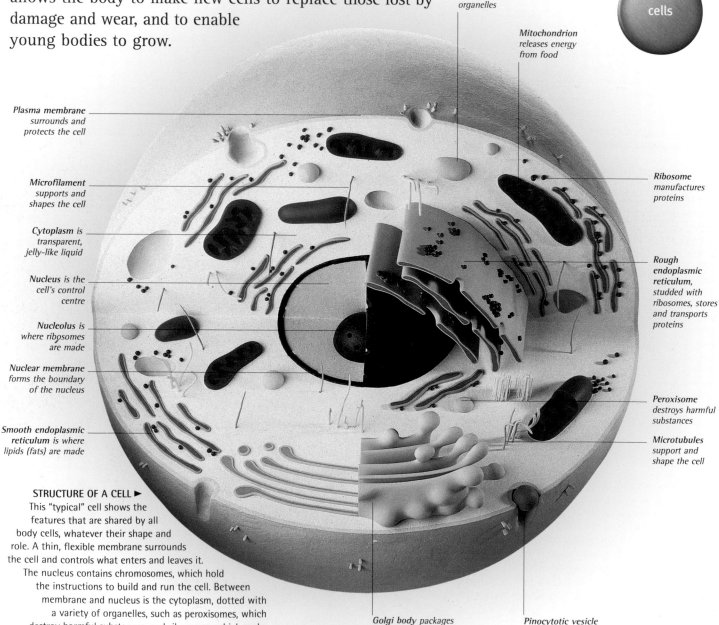

Lysosome breaks down worn-out organelles

Mitochondrion releases energy from food

cells

Plasma membrane surrounds and protects the cell

Microfilament supports and shapes the cell

Cytoplasm is transparent, jelly-like liquid

Nucleus is the cell's control centre

Nucleolus is where ribosomes are made

Nuclear membrane forms the boundary of the nucleus

Smooth endoplasmic reticulum is where lipids (fats) are made

Ribosome manufactures proteins

Rough endoplasmic reticulum, studded with ribosomes, stores and transports proteins

Peroxisome destroys harmful substances

Microtubules support and shape the cell

STRUCTURE OF A CELL ▶
This "typical" cell shows the features that are shared by all body cells, whatever their shape and role. A thin, flexible membrane surrounds the cell and controls what enters and leaves it. The nucleus contains chromosomes, which hold the instructions to build and run the cell. Between membrane and nucleus is the cytoplasm, dotted with a variety of organelles, such as peroxisomes, which destroy harmful substances, and ribosomes, which make proteins. Each one contributes to bringing the cell to life.

Golgi body packages substances made by the cell

Pinocytotic vesicle takes liquid to the cell

## HOW CELLS DIVIDE

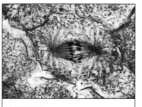

**PREPARING FOR DIVISION**
Cell division creates two "daughter" cells, identical to the "parent" that produced them. The nucleus of the parent cell contains 46 chromosomes, which contain instructions for operating and building the cell. Before cell division begins, each thread-like chromosome shrinks and copies itself so it consists of two linked identical strands.

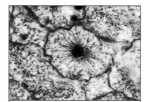

**MITOSIS**
The next stage, called mitosis, is when the two copies of each chromosome separate and each strand becomes a chromosome in its own right. The new chromosomes (black) are pulled to opposite ends of the cell by microtubules (red threads) so that each end has 46 chromosomes that are identical to those at the other end.

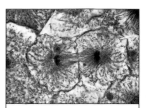

**NEW CELLS SEPARATE**
As mitosis ends, each new set of chromosomes becomes enclosed within its own nucleus. A nuclear membrane reforms and the cytoplasm divides to form two separate cells with identical chromosomes and organelles. The whole process ensures that the new cells, whether for growth or repair, function as they should.

*Fat cell dominated by droplet of fat inside*

### ◄ FAT TISSUE

Fat provides the body with one of its sources of energy and is stored in fat cells, or adipocytes. Most of the cell is occupied by a droplet of fat, so much so that the nucleus is pushed to one side. Groups of fat cells form adipose tissue. As well as acting as an energy store, the layer of adipose tissue under the skin insulates the body against heat loss. It also supports and protects organs such as the kidneys and eyeballs.

*Neuron contains the nucleus*

*Dendrite are thread-like links between cells*

### HOW LONG DOES A CELL LIVE?

| CELL TYPE | FUNCTION | LIFE SPAN |
|---|---|---|
| Small intestine cell | Absorbing food | 36 hours |
| White blood cell | Killing invaders | 13 days |
| Red blood cell | Transporting oxygen | 120 days |
| Liver cell | Part of the body's chemical factory | 500 days |
| Nerve cell | Relaying messages | up to 100 years |

### NERVE CELLS ►

This micrograph shows two of the billions of neurons or nerve cells that form the nervous system. Neurons pass on electrical signals, called nerve impulses, at high speeds to control body activities. Each neuron has a cell body with thread-like dendrites that bring in nerve impulses from other neurons. Axons, or nerve fibres, transmit nerve impulses away from the cell body over distances of up to 1 m (3¼ ft).

*Axon extends from nerve body*

*Head of sperm cell contains payload of chromosomes*

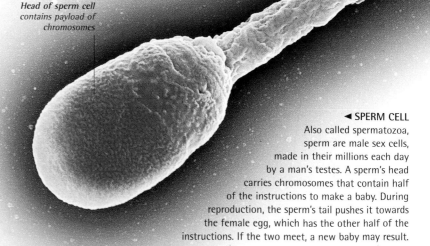

### ▲ EGG CELL

One of the largest cells in the body, an egg, or ovum, is a spherical cell about 0.1 mm across. Eggs are female sex cells, produced by the ovaries in their millions before birth. They remain dormant until the teenage years after which they are released, usually one by one each month. Like sperm, eggs contain half of the instructions to produce a baby. But unlike the streamlined and much smaller sperm, eggs cannot move by themselves.

### ◄ SPERM CELL

Also called spermatozoa, sperm are male sex cells, made in their millions each day by a man's testes. A sperm's head carries chromosomes that contain half of the instructions to make a baby. During reproduction, the sperm's tail pushes it towards the female egg, which has the other half of the instructions. If the two meet, a new baby may result.

# BODY CONSTRUCTION

The body is organized on five different levels, beginning with simple body cells and progressing through tissues, organs, and systems to the most complex level, the body itself. Groups of similar cells make up body tissues and two or more tissues together make an organ, such as the stomach or the heart. Organs and tissues that work together to carry out a body function – such as digestion – make up the body's 12 separate systems. These systems do not operate in isolation but rely on each other to keep the body going.

body systems

| MAJOR BODY ORGANS | | |
|---|---|---|
| *BODY SYSTEM* | *ORGAN* | *ADULT SIZE* |
| Nervous system | Brain | 1.45–1.6 kg (3¼–3½ lb) |
| Skeletal | Femur length | 40–45 cm (15–18 in) |
| Circulatory | Heart mass | 250–350 g (9–12 oz) |
| Digestive | Liver | 1.4 kg (3 lb) |
| Endocrine | Pituitary gland diameter | 1–1.5 cm (³⁄₈–⁵⁄₈ in) |
| Respiratory | Lung mass | 0.5 kg (1¼ lb) |
| Urinary | Bladder volume (full) | 700–800 ml (1¼–1½ pt) |
| Integumentary | Skin mass | 4–5 kg (9–11 lb) |

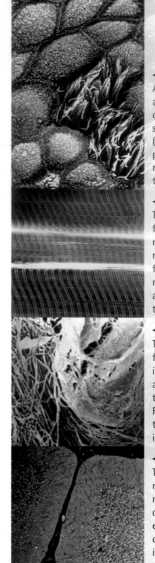

◄ EPITHELIAL TISSUE
Also called epithelium, epithelial tissue covers and protects the body and also lines hollow organs and cavities inside. This magnified image shows epithelial tissue lining the trachea (windpipe). It consists of a sheet of tightly packed cells, which forms a barrier to invading micro-organisms. Epithelial cells divide constantly to replace those lost through wear and tear.

◄ MUSCLE TISSUE
The cells that make up muscular tissue, called fibres, contract or shorten when stimulated by nerve signals. Skeletal muscle (shown here) moves the body. It has long striated (striped) fibres and is attached to the skeleton. Cardiac muscle, found only in the heart, pumps blood around the body. Smooth muscle is found in the walls of hollow organs and alters their shape.

◄ CONNECTIVE TISSUE
The most diverse of tissues, connective tissues form a framework that supports, protects, and insulates the body, and holds it together. Types are found in cartilage and bone, which form the skeleton, and also in tendons and ligaments. Fibres of collagen (shown here) give connective tissues strength and flexibility. Other types include fat-storing adipose tissue and blood.

◄ NERVOUS TISSUE
The body's major communication and control network – the brain, spinal cord, and nerves – is made of nervous tissue. Nervous tissue consists of nerve cells, or neurons, which transmit electrical signals called nerve impulses, and glial cells that support the neurons. The image (left) is of a section of nervous tissue in the cerebellum, a part of the brain that co-ordinates movement.

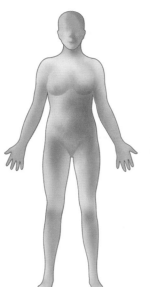

▲ INTEGUMENTARY
This system provides the body's outer covering and consists of skin, hair, and nails. Skin forms a waterproof barrier, which stops the body dehydrating and helps regulate its temperature. It shields the body from harmful UV rays in sunlight and disease-causing micro-organisms.

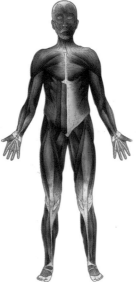

▲ MUSCULAR
The muscular system consists of 640 or so skeletal muscles that are able to contract, or get shorter, pulling on bones across flexible joints to move the body. Muscles are organized in layers that overlap in intricate patterns. They are attached to bones by tough tendons.

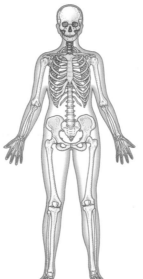

▲ SKELETAL
The skeletal system is a strong, flexible framework of bones, cartilage, and ligaments. This shapes and supports the body, surrounds and protects internal organs, such as the brain, and allows the body to move. Bones also store minerals such as calcium and make blood cells.

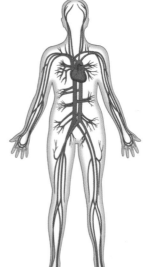

▲ CIRCULATORY
The circulatory system consists of the heart, a network of blood vessels, and the blood that flows through them. It delivers food, oxygen, and other essentials to all body cells and removes their wastes. It also helps the body maintain its temperature and fight infection.

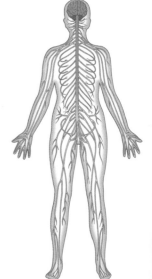

▲ NERVOUS
The nervous system is the body's main control system. The brain and spinal cord, which make up the central nervous system (CNS), process and store incoming information, and send out instructions to nerves. These ferry signals between the CNS and the rest of the body.

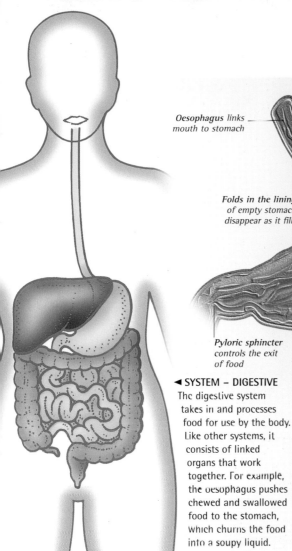

Oesophagus links mouth to stomach

Folds in the lining of empty stomach disappear as it fills

Pyloric sphincter controls the exit of food

Muscle layers contract to churn food inside

### ◄ SYSTEM – DIGESTIVE

The digestive system takes in and processes food for use by the body. Like other systems, it consists of linked organs that work together. For example, the oesophagus pushes chewed and swallowed food to the stomach, which churns the food into a soupy liquid.

### ▲ ORGAN – STOMACH

As part of the digestive system, the stomach stores chewed food and partially digests it. Like other organs – such as the kidneys in the urinary system – it has a recognizable shape and consists of a variety of tissues. Some tissues, for example, enable the stomach to contract. Others supply blood or nerve stimulation, or form the stomach's inner lining.

### ▲ TISSUE – MUCOSA

Seen under a microscope, this is a section through the folded lining of the stomach, also called the mucosa or mucous membrane. It consists of three of the types of tissues that form the stomach. Covering the surface is a thin layer of epithelial tissue. Under this is a thicker layer of connective tissue, below which is the mucosa's smooth muscle layer.

### ▲ CELLS – EPITHELIAL

This micrograph shows the surface of cells in epithelial tissue, lining the stomach. The tight junctions between the cells prevent corrosive stomach juices from reaching the connective tissue below and also secrete mucus, which coats and protects the cells. The cells are surrounding the entrance to a gastric gland, which produces digestive juices.

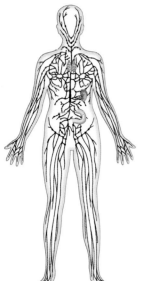

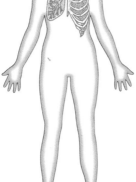

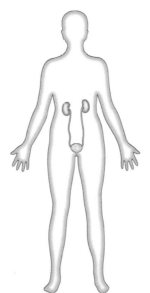

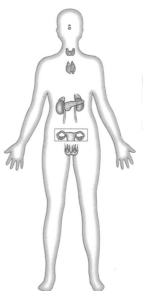

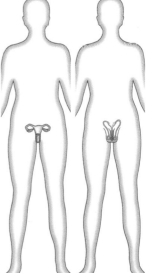

### ▲ LYMPHATIC AND IMMUNE

The lymphatic system drains excess fluid, called lymph, from tissues, filters it to remove pathogens (disease-causing micro-organisms) and debris, and returns it to the blood. The immune system consists of cells called lymphocytes that help protect the body from infection.

### ▲ RESPIRATORY

The respiratory system, made up of the respiratory tract and the lungs, supplies the body with oxygen, which is needed by all cells to release energy. Breathing moves air in and out of the lungs, where oxygen passes into the blood and waste carbon dioxide is expelled.

### ▲ URINARY

The urinary system consists of the kidneys, ureters, bladder, and urethra. The kidneys process blood passing through them, removing excess water and potentially harmful waste products, such as urea. These then pass out of the body through the urethra as urine.

### ▲ ENDOCRINE

The endocrine system controls many body processes, including growth, reproduction, and metabolism. It consists of glands that release chemicals called hormones into the bloodstream. These hormones travel to, and alter the activities of, specific tissues under their control.

### ▲ REPRODUCTIVE

This system enables a man and a woman to produce children. The female and male systems differ, but both begin to function in the early teenage years. A woman produces eggs, which, if fertilized by a male sperm, may develop into a baby within the woman's uterus.

# SKELETAL FRAMEWORK

Constructed from bones, cartilage, and ligaments, the skeleton provides a strong, flexible framework that supports the body, protects internal organs, and produces movement when pulled by muscles. Bones, which make up about 20 per cent of the body's mass, also produce blood cells and store calcium, essential for strong teeth. Tough and flexible cartilage covers bone ends in joints and forms the framework of the nose and ear. Ligaments are strong "straps" that hold the bones of the skeleton together.

*Skull surrounds the brain and forms the face*

*Mandible (lower jaw)*

*Scapula (shoulder blade) forms joint with the humerus*

*Clavicle (collar bone)*

*Sternum (breast bone) forms a plate that protects the heart*

*Humerus is the upper arm bone*

*Spinal cord runs downwards from brain within backbone*

*Ribs surround and protect heart and lungs*

*Backbone (spine) is flexible column of vertebrae*

*Process of vertebra provides anchorage for muscles*

*Metacarpals are bones in the palm of the hand*

*Pelvic (hip) girdle supports the abdominal organs*

*Phalanges are the finger bones*

*Carpals (wrist bones)*

*Radius is a bone of the forearm*

*Ulna is inner bone of the forearm*

*Fibula is the lower leg bone behind the shin bone (tibia)*

*Femur (thigh bone) is the body's largest bone*

*Calcaneus (heel bone)*

*Vertebra is one of the bones of spine*

*Intevertebral disc is pad of cartilage between vertebrae*

## ◀ BACKBONE
Seen in side view in this MRI scan, the backbone forms the body's main axis, supporting the head and trunk. Extending from skull to pelvis, it is a tower of 24 bones called vertebrae, with a further nine fused to form the sacrum and coccyx at its base. Cartilage discs between vertebrae allow flexibility, while the tunnel they form surrounds and protects the spinal cord, which carries nerve impulses to and from the brain. The backbone's S-shape adds strength, absorbs shock, and balances the upper body.

## SKELETON ▶
The 206 bones of the skeleton can be divided into two groups. The 80 bones of the axial skeleton – the backbone, ribs, and skull – run down the middle of the body and form its core. The 126 bones of the appendicular skeleton – the arm bones, shoulder girdle, hip girdle, and leg bones – "hang off" the axial skeleton and allow a wide range of movements. Arm and hand bones manipulate objects, while leg and foot bones support and move the body's weight.

## RADIONUCLIDE SCAN

These radionuclide scans of a healthy skeleton reveal which areas of bone tissue are more active than others. When a small amount of radionuclide, a chemical that gives off radioactive gamma rays, is injected into the body it is taken up by bone cells. The more active the cells, the more radionuclide they take up, and the more gamma rays they give off. Gamma rays are detected by a gamma camera linked to a computer, which produces the type of images shown here. Areas of high activity ("hot spots") appear red, while areas of low activity ("cold spots") appear blue. The scan also detects areas of unusually high activity, which may be caused by cancer, infection, or injury.

High | BONE ACTIVITY | Low

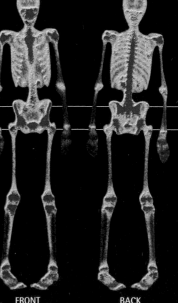

FRONT          BACK

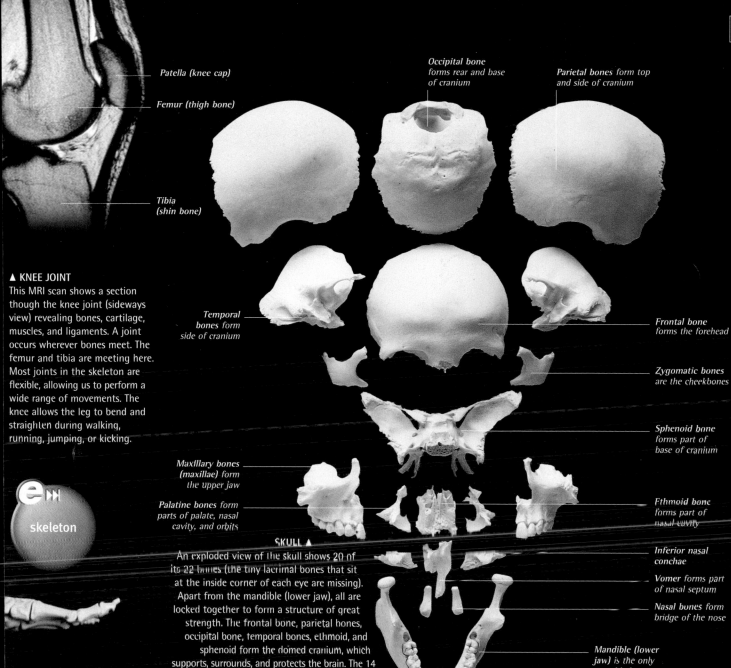

Patella (knee cap)

Femur (thigh bone)

Tibia (shin bone)

Occipital bone forms rear and base of cranium

Parietal bones form top and side of cranium

Temporal bones form side of cranium

Frontal bone forms the forehead

Zygomatic bones are the cheekbones

Sphenoid bone forms part of base of cranium

Maxillary bones (maxillae) form the upper jaw

Palatine bones form parts of palate, nasal cavity, and orbits

Ethmoid bone forms part of nasal cavity

Inferior nasal conchae

Vomer forms part of nasal septum

Nasal bones form bridge of the nose

Mandible (lower jaw) is the only movable bone

## ▲ KNEE JOINT

This MRI scan shows a section though the knee joint (sideways view) revealing bones, cartilage, muscles, and ligaments. A joint occurs wherever bones meet. The femur and tibia are meeting here. Most joints in the skeleton are flexible, allowing us to perform a wide range of movements. The knee allows the leg to bend and straighten during walking, running, jumping, or kicking.

skeleton

### SKULL ▲

An exploded view of the skull shows 20 of its 22 bones (the tiny lacrimal bones that sit at the inside corner of each eye are missing). Apart from the mandible (lower jaw), all are locked together to form a structure of great strength. The frontal bone, parietal bones, occipital bone, temporal bones, ethmoid, and sphenoid form the domed cranium, which supports, surrounds, and protects the brain. The 14 facial bones provide a framework for the face and anchor the muscles that produce facial expressions.

Patella (knee cap) protects the knee

Tibia (shin bone) carries most of the weight of the lower leg

Tarsals (ankle bones) include the large calcaneus

Metatarsals are five long bones between ankle and toes

Phalanges (toe bones)

## FACE RECONSTRUCTION

### ARCHAEOLOGICAL FIND
Bones and teeth are the only parts of the body that survive long after death. This skull fragment has been excavated from an ancient site during an archaeological dig. Old skeletons can reveal much about the diet, lifestyle, or disease history of someone who died long ago. But a skull can be used to re-create a person's facial features.

### PLASTER-CAST SKULL
The first part of the process of facial reconstruction is to clean the skull and make a plaster cast of it. Then the parts that are missing have to be restored. Reconstructing the face is the job of a forensic sculptor – someone who uses both scientific and artistic skills to rebuild the head using clues provided by the skull.

### REBUILDING MUSCLE
The appearance of head and face depends on the shape of the skull and the muscles that overlie it. Sculptors use their anatomical knowledge to form muscles from clay to cover the "bones" in the plaster cast skull. The depth of the facial and cranial muscles is determined using pegs, as can be seen above.

### FINISHING TOUCH
Once the skull has been "fleshed out" with muscle, the finishing touch is to add a clay "skin" to form a recognizable face. Reconstructed faces such as these are not just used by archaeologists to visualize ancient people. Forensic sculptors are also used by the police to help identify the remains of murder victims.

# BONES AND FRACTURES

Bones are moist, living organs made of hard bone tissue, blood vessels, and nerves. Bone tissue consists of a matrix of calcium salts, which give bone its hardness, collagen fibres, which provide strength and flexibility, and cells that maintain the bony matrix. Bone tissue is denser on the outside of a bone than inside. This arrangement makes bones both strong and light: weight-for-weight six times stronger than a piece of steel. Despite their remarkable strength, bones sometimes fracture or break, but they also repair themselves. As well as supporting the body, bones also make blood cells and store the mineral calcium.

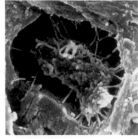

**▲ OSTEOBLAST CELL**
Bone is made by cells called osteoblasts. As they lay down bone matrix, osteoblasts become isolated and turn into mature bone cells called osteocytes, like this one, which are stranded inside their own space or lacuna. Osteocytes maintain bone tissue.

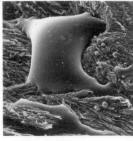

**▲ OSTEOCLAST CELL**
Bones are constantly being reshaped in response to the stresses upon them. Osteoclasts (above, gold) break down bone; osteoblasts rebuild it. These cells help control calcium levels in blood by releasing calcium into the blood or returning it to its bony store.

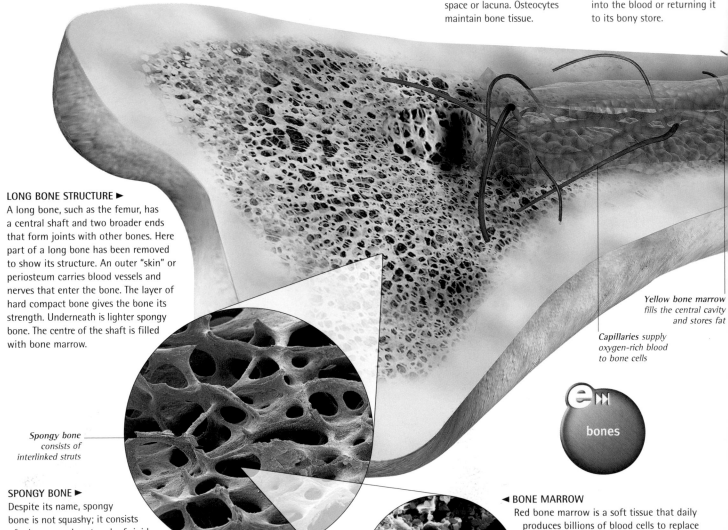

**LONG BONE STRUCTURE ▶**
A long bone, such as the femur, has a central shaft and two broader ends that form joints with other bones. Here part of a long bone has been removed to show its structure. An outer "skin" or periosteum carries blood vessels and nerves that enter the bone. The layer of hard compact bone gives the bone its strength. Underneath is lighter spongy bone. The centre of the shaft is filled with bone marrow.

*Yellow bone marrow fills the central cavity and stores fat*

*Capillaries supply oxygen-rich blood to bone cells*

*Spongy bone consists of interlinked struts*

**SPONGY BONE ▶**
Despite its name, spongy bone is not squashy; it consists of a honeycomb network of rigid struts, called trabeculae, with spaces between them. This arrangement of struts makes spongy bone both lightweight and strong. If an entire bone were made of compact bone, the skeleton would be too heavy to move. The combination of denser compact bone with lighter spongy bone allows bones to bear heavy loads and stresses while reducing the overall weight.

*Red blood cells, newly produced by red bone marrow*

**◀ BONE MARROW**
Red bone marrow is a soft tissue that daily produces billions of blood cells to replace those that have worn out. In babies, red bone marrow is found in spongy bone cavities and in the central cavities of long bones. In the teen years, much of this red marrow is replaced by yellow marrow, which acts as a fat store. In adults, blood cell production is restricted to the red marrow in the head (top end) of the femur and humerus, and in the spongy bone of flat bones such as the scapula.

**e⏩ bones**

## ◄ OSTEONS IN COMPACT BONE

Seen here in cross-section is an osteon, or Haversian system, one of the many cylindrical units that make up hard, compact bone. Clearly visible are concentric tubes made of bone matrix; these are the lamellae that make up each osteon. The dotted, tiny spaces between the lamellae are called lacunae and these contain osteocytes, which help to maintain bone tissue. At the centre of each osteon is a hollow channel called the Haversian canal, which carries blood vessels and nerves (both shown in red here). Osteons are arranged in parallel along the bone, acting as dense weight-bearing pillars that make the outside of each bone both hard and strong.

*Hollow channel carries blood vessels and nerves*

*Lacunae contain osteocytes that help to maintain bone tissue*

## WEIGHTLESSNESS

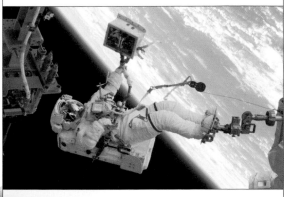

An astronaut can float in space because he or she is virtually weightless, not subject to the full force of gravity. On Earth, gravity pulls us downwards, giving our bodies weight. When we walk, run, or jump our bones resist the stresses produced by moving our body weight, continually reshaping themselves to make sure that the skeleton is strong enough to support the body.

But in space, far away from Earth's surface, there is little gravity. No longer needed to support body weight, bones lose up to one per cent of their mass each month. On return to Earth after a long spell in space, astronaut's bones are more likely to fracture – a problem that makes longer space missions, such as a three-year journey to Mars, impossible.

*Incus or anvil, a tiny bone found inside the ear*

*Vein carries oxygen-poor blood away from bone cells*

*Osteon is one of the cylindrical units that make up compact bone*

*Periosteum is a thin layer of fibrous tissue that covers the bone*

*Compact bone is the hard, dense outer layer of bone*

## ▲ SMALLEST BONE

Fitting on a fingertip, the incus (anvil) is one of three linked ossicles or ear bones, the smallest bones in the body. The other two are the malleus (hammer) and, even smaller, the stapes (stirrup), just 5-mm (¼-in) long. The ossicles are located inside a cavity within the temporal bones on each side of the skull. They transmit sounds to the innermost part of the ear.

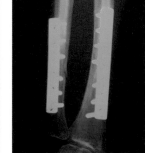

## ▲ FIXING FRACTURES

The X-ray (above, left) shows a serious fracture of the lower arm bones, the radius and ulna, where the broken ends have separated. Fractures are treated by lining up the broken ends, then immobilizing the body part with a plaster or plastic cast so that the bone ends are held firmly together and do not move. In the fracture shown above right, steel pins and plates have also been used to hold bones in the correct positions during healing.

## HOW BONES HEAL THEMSELVES

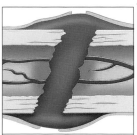

### BLOOD CLOT FORMATION
Within hours of a fracture, the broken bone has started to repair itself. A blood clot forms between the broken ends, as this section through a fractured long bone shows. This clot seals off torn blood vessels in the bone and periosteum and stops them bleeding into the wound. The fracture site is swollen and painful.

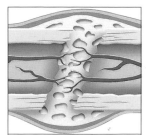

### CALLUS FORMATION
Within days of the injury, the periosteum has reformed, and the blood clot has been replaced by a callus of soft fibrous tissue. Three to four weeks after the injury, as blood vessels grow into the callus, osteoblasts (bone-making cells) convert the fibrous tissue into a spongy bone callus. This reunites the broken ends.

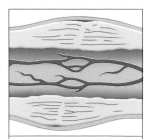

### NEW BONE FORMATION
Within months of the fracture, the repair is almost complete. Bone cells reshape the bony callus to form a new central marrow cavity. They also remove the "bulge" around the callus and lay down tough compact bone to reinforce the walls of the bone's shaft, so that the bone retains its original shape.

# MOVING PARTS

The skeleton is not a rigid structure – its bones meet at joints, which provide stability by holding bones together, and flexibility by allowing movement. There are three types of joint: fixed, semi-movable, and synovial. Fixed joints allow no movement, while semi-movable joints permit a limited degree. Most of the body's 400 joints are freely movable, synovial joints found in, for example, the knee or finger. Cartilage is also found in joints. Hyaline cartilage covers bone ends in synovial joints, while fibrocartilage is found in semi-movable and fixed joints.

*Bone* meets another bone at joint

*Periosteum* covers surface of bone shaft

*Synovial membrane* produces synovial fluid

*Synovial fluid* fills the space between bones

*Hyaline cartilage* covers the bone ends

*Fibrous capsule* holds the joint together

◄ SYNOVIAL JOINT
Within these freely movable joints, bone ends are covered with slippery hyaline cartilage and are separated by a space filled with oily synovial fluid. This combination allows the joint to move with less friction than two ice cubes sliding over each other. A fibrous joint capsule holds the bones together in the joint, often reinforced by strap-like ligaments surrounding it. Inside the capsule, the synovial membrane secretes synovial fluid.

*Skull* has only one synovial joint – where the lower jaw is attached

◄ TYPES OF SYNOVIAL JOINTS IN THE BODY
The body's synovial joints are divided into six types – ball and socket, ellipsoidal, hinge, pivot, plane, and saddle – according to the shapes of the bone ends and the way they fit together in a joint. This also determines the range of movement a joint permits. For example, the ball and socket joint at the shoulder allows movement in most directions, while the elbow – a hinge joint – allows only movement back and forth in one direction. The box (far left) uses simple diagrams to show how each type of joint works, and includes a colour key for the skeleton below.

## SYNOVIAL JOINT KEY

**BALL AND SOCKET JOINT**
Found in the shoulder (between humerus and pectoral girdle) and in the hip (between femur and pelvic girdle), this joint allows the greatest range of movement. The ball-like head of one bone fits into the cup-shaped socket of another, allowing rotation in any direction.

**ELLIPSOIDAL JOINT**
The oval, domed end of one bone fits into an oval cavity on another, allowing movement from side to side and back and forth. These joints are found in the wrist – between the radius and carpals – and at the base of the fingers.

**HINGE JOINT**
Found in elbows, knees, fingers, and toes, hinge joints allow movement in just one plane to either straighten or bend a body part. The cylindrical end of one bone fits into the grooved surface of the other, an arrangement that prevents any side to side movement.

**PIVOT JOINT**
In a pivot joint, the end of one bone rotates in a round space in another. For example, in the neck, a projection from the second vertebra fits into a space in the first, allowing the head to turn from side to side.

**PLANE JOINT**
Where bones meet in plane (gliding) joints, their almost flat surfaces are held tightly together. This permits only short sliding movements from side to side. The joint between the wrist bones in the hand is a plane joint.

**SADDLE JOINT**
The saddle joint consists of two U-shaped surfaces positioned at right angles to each other, like a rider sitting on a saddle. At the base of the thumb, this joint allows the thumb to rotate in all directions.

## FIXED JOINT ▶

If the bones that make up the skull moved, they would damage the brain, so they are locked together by fixed, immovable joints called sutures. The jagged edges of the skull bones fit together like the pieces of a jigsaw. A thin layer of fibrous tissue reinforces each suture. By middle age, this fibrous tissue has been replaced by bone, and neighbouring bones are fused.

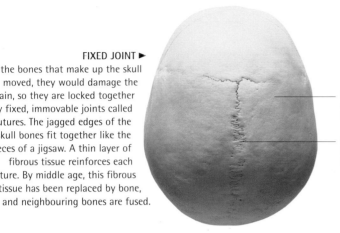

*Parietal bone – one of two on top of the skull*

*Sagittal suture, between left and right parietal bones*

### MAKING ARTIFICIAL CARTILAGE

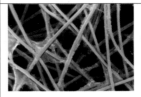 

GROWING CARTILAGE   BIOREACTOR IN ACTION

Scientists can now make artificial cartilage to replace cartilage lost from the bone ends in joints through wear, disease, or injury. A patient's own cartilage cells are cultured (grown) on a network of synthetic fibres (above, left). This takes place in a bioreactor (above, right), which rotates to ensure that all cartilage cells receive enough nutrients and the cartilage grows evenly. Artificial cartilage is then implanted on the bone ends in the defective joint. The synthetic fibres break down, leaving behind only natural cartilage tissue.

## ◀ SEMI-MOVABLE JOINT

As their name suggests, these joints permit only limited movement – an example being the inter-vertebral discs between the backbone's vertebrae (shown left). However, together the movements of the vertebrae give the backbone flexibility, allowing it to bend backwards, forwards, and sideways. Made of fibrocartilage with a soft centre, the discs also act as shock absorbers when we walk or run.

*Intervertebral disc links vertebrae in a semi-movable joint*

*Vertebra forms part of backbone*

## ▲ DISLOCATED JOINT

When a joint is dislocated, bones are forced out of line by, for example, a sports injury or a fall. Knuckles, shown in this X-ray of a finger, are often dislocated, as is the shoulder joint. Dislocation may tear the ligaments that hold the joint together, damaging the capsule around the joint, and causing pain, swelling, and bruising. Treatment involves a doctor manipulating the bones back into their correct position.

## ◀ JOINT REPLACEMENT

The protective cartilage that covers bone ends in a joint can wear away through disease or injury. As cartilage reduces friction, its loss causes pain and immobility. Worn-out joints can be replaced by artificial implants, as this X-ray of the knee shows. The replacement joint is attached to the femur and tibia.

*Artificial hinge joint in knee*

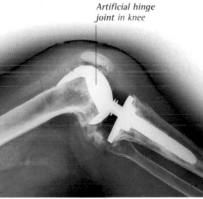

*Hands have many joints, making them flexible and versatile*

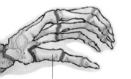

*Knee joint is the largest and most complex in the body*

*Hinge joint in ankle allows foot to be pointed up and down*

*Foot joints provide strong, flexible platform for movement*

joints

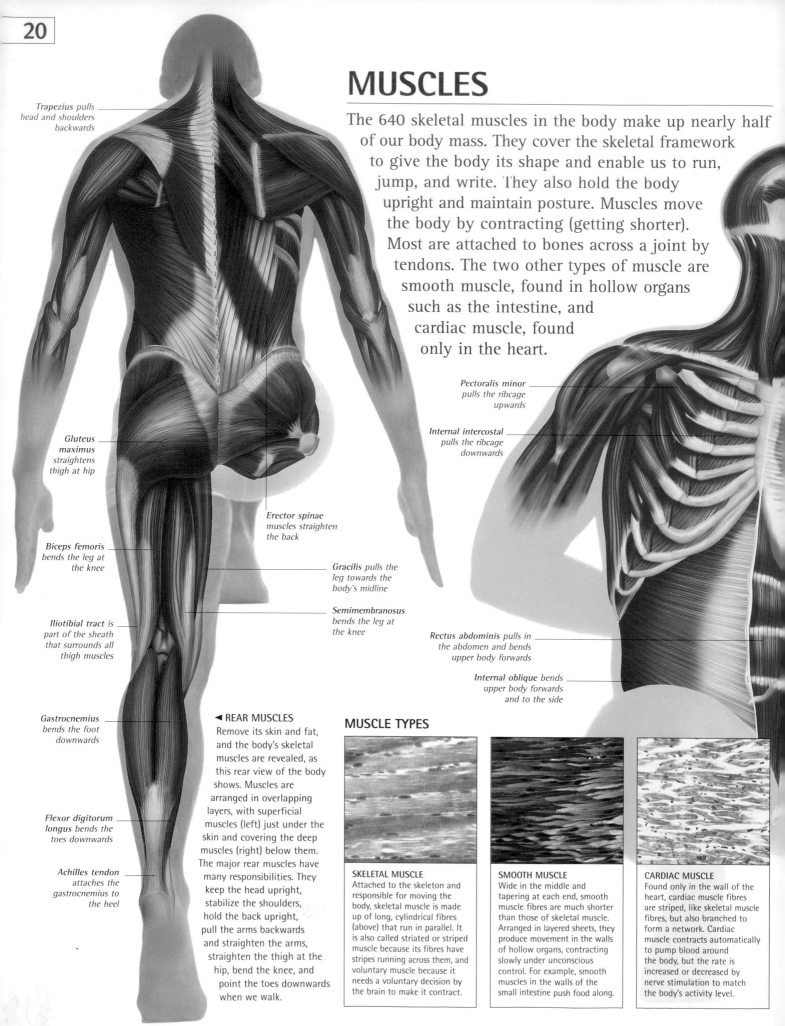

*Trapezius* pulls head and shoulders backwards

*Gluteus maximus* straightens thigh at hip

*Biceps femoris* bends the leg at the knee

*Iliotibial tract* is part of the sheath that surrounds all thigh muscles

*Gastrocnemius* bends the foot downwards

*Flexor digitorum longus* bends the toes downwards

*Achilles tendon* attaches the gastrocnemius to the heel

*Erector spinae* muscles straighten the back

*Gracilis* pulls the leg towards the body's midline

*Semimembranosus* bends the leg at the knee

# MUSCLES

The 640 skeletal muscles in the body make up nearly half of our body mass. They cover the skeletal framework to give the body its shape and enable us to run, jump, and write. They also hold the body upright and maintain posture. Muscles move the body by contracting (getting shorter). Most are attached to bones across a joint by tendons. The two other types of muscle are smooth muscle, found in hollow organs such as the intestine, and cardiac muscle, found only in the heart.

*Pectoralis minor* pulls the ribcage upwards

*Internal intercostal* pulls the ribcage downwards

*Rectus abdominis* pulls in the abdomen and bends upper body forwards

*Internal oblique* bends upper body forwards and to the side

### ◄ REAR MUSCLES
Remove its skin and fat, and the body's skeletal muscles are revealed, as this rear view of the body shows. Muscles are arranged in overlapping layers, with superficial muscles (left) just under the skin and covering the deep muscles (right) below them. The major rear muscles have many responsibilities. They keep the head upright, stabilize the shoulders, hold the back upright, pull the arms backwards and straighten the arms, straighten the thigh at the hip, bend the knee, and point the toes downwards when we walk.

## MUSCLE TYPES

**SKELETAL MUSCLE**
Attached to the skeleton and responsible for moving the body, skeletal muscle is made up of long, cylindrical fibres (above) that run in parallel. It is also called striated or striped muscle because its fibres have stripes running across them, and voluntary muscle because it needs a voluntary decision by the brain to make it contract.

**SMOOTH MUSCLE**
Wide in the middle and tapering at each end, smooth muscle fibres are much shorter than those of skeletal muscle. Arranged in layered sheets, they produce movement in the walls of hollow organs, contracting slowly under unconscious control. For example, smooth muscles in the walls of the small intestine push food along.

**CARDIAC MUSCLE**
Found only in the wall of the heart, cardiac muscle fibres are striped, like skeletal muscle fibres, but also branched to form a network. Cardiac muscle contracts automatically to pump blood around the body, but the rate is increased or decreased by nerve stimulation to match the body's activity level.

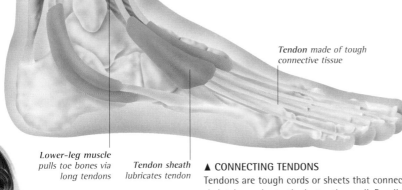

*Tendon made of tough connective tissue*

*Lower-leg muscle pulls toe bones via long tendons*

*Tendon sheath lubricates tendon*

*Orbicularis oculi closes the eyelids*

*Masseter pulls lower jaw upwards during chewing*

*Orbicularis oris purses the lips*

*Depressor anguli oris draws the corners of the mouth downwards*

## ▲ CONNECTING TENDONS

Tendons are tough cords or sheets that connect skeletal muscles to the bones they pull. Bundles of tough collagen fibres run in parallel inside tendons to give them great tensile (pulling) strength. Each tendon is an extension of the connective tissue around a muscle and is embedded in the outer part of a bone, anchoring its muscle firmly in place. Many muscles responsible for toe and finger movements are located in the lower leg and arm, respectively, and have very long tendons that extend to foot or hand bones. Sheaths surround and lubricate these tendons to make them slide smoothly.

## ELECTRICAL STIMULATION

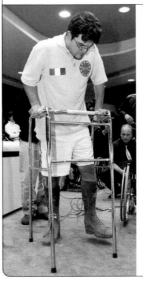

Walking is a complex process that involves the contraction of different leg muscles in a precise order when they receive electrical signals from the brain via the spinal cord.

A spinal cord injury (SCI) prevents these signals from reaching leg muscles. But researchers are investigating ways of using artificial electrical stimulation to help people with SCI, like Rafael (left). The electrodes attached to Rafael's legs are electrically stimulating his leg muscles to contract, enabling him to take a few steps.

This technique has yet to be perfected. The challenge is to mimic the brain to ensure that the electrodes stimulate muscles to contract in the right sequence.

*Deltoid raises the arm sideways, backwards, and forwards*

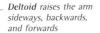

muscles

*Pectoralis major pulls arm forwards and into the body*

*Triceps brachii straightens arm at the elbow*

*Biceps brachii bends the arm at the elbow*

*Deep flexor of fingers bends the fingers*

*External oblique bends upper body forwards and to the side*

*Sartorius turns the leg and bends it at the hip*

*Quadriceps femoris straightens the leg at the knee*

## ▼ MAINTAINING POSTURE

This man uses his skeletal muscles not to move but to keep his body fixed in a yoga position. This illustrates the fact that muscles not only move the body but also maintain posture when, for example, we sit or stand. To maintain posture, muscles shorten only slightly yet still exert a powerful pull. This partial contraction produces a firmness called muscle tone that prevents the body collapsing under the force of gravity. Only when we sleep does muscle tone decrease, explaining why a seated person's head falls to one side when they become drowsy.

*Deltoid tenses to hold arm in position below the body*

*Triceps brachii tenses to hold arm in partially extended position*

## MUSCLE FACTS

| MUSCLE | LOCATION | FEATURE | SIZE/MASS |
|---|---|---|---|
| Sartorius | Thigh | Longest | 50 cm (20 in) |
| Stapedius | Ear | Shortest | 0.5 cm (¼ in) |
| External oblique | Abdomen | Widest | 45 cm (18 in) |
| Masseter | Jaw | Strongest | 550 N force |
| Gluteus maximus | Buttock | Bulkiest | 1 kg (2¼ lb) |
| Erector spinae | Back | Longest group | 90 cm (3 ft) |

## ▲ FRONT MUSCLES

This image shows the major muscles of the front of the body – the deep muscles on the left and superficial muscles on the right. The front muscles produce facial expressions, bend the head forwards and to the side, move the arms outwards and forwards and bend them at the elbow, bend the trunk forwards and to the side, bend the leg at the hip, straighten the knee when running or walking, and lift the foot upwards. Front and rear muscles have Latin names that describe features such as size, location, shape, or action.

*Soleus bends foot downwards*

*Connective tissue band holds long tendons in place*

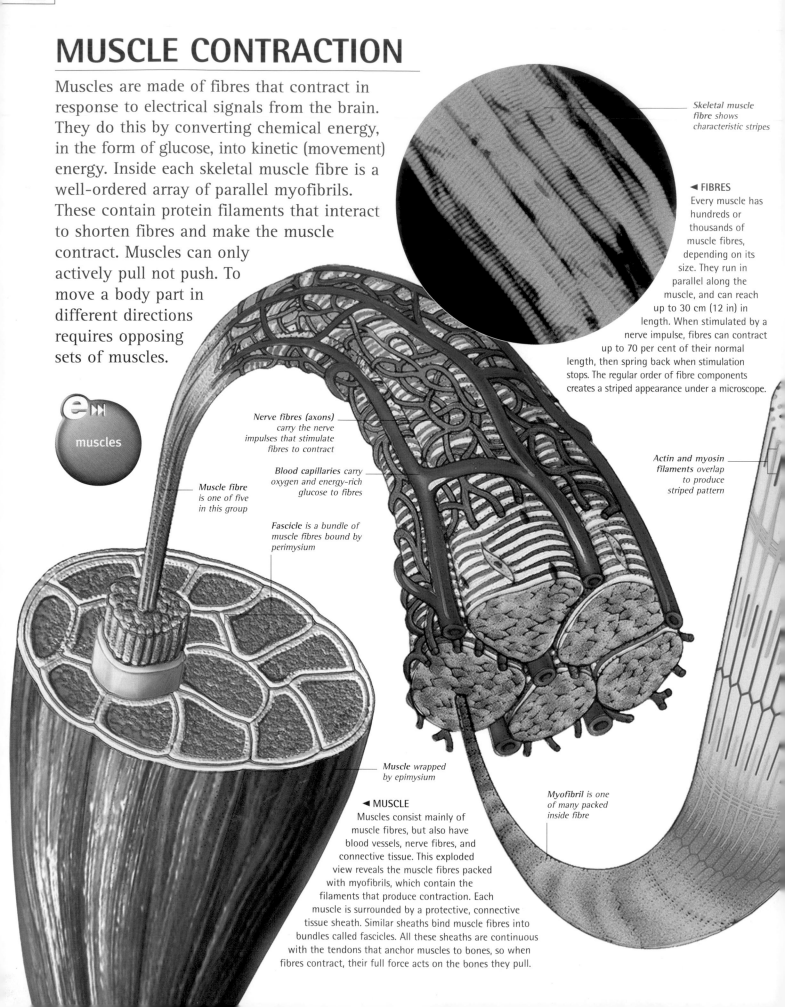

# MUSCLE CONTRACTION

Muscles are made of fibres that contract in response to electrical signals from the brain. They do this by converting chemical energy, in the form of glucose, into kinetic (movement) energy. Inside each skeletal muscle fibre is a well-ordered array of parallel myofibrils. These contain protein filaments that interact to shorten fibres and make the muscle contract. Muscles can only actively pull not push. To move a body part in different directions requires opposing sets of muscles.

muscles

*Skeletal muscle fibre shows characteristic stripes*

◄ FIBRES
Every muscle has hundreds or thousands of muscle fibres, depending on its size. They run in parallel along the muscle, and can reach up to 30 cm (12 in) in length. When stimulated by a nerve impulse, fibres can contract up to 70 per cent of their normal length, then spring back when stimulation stops. The regular order of fibre components creates a striped appearance under a microscope.

*Nerve fibres (axons) carry the nerve impulses that stimulate fibres to contract*

*Blood capillaries carry oxygen and energy-rich glucose to fibres*

*Actin and myosin filaments overlap to produce striped pattern*

*Muscle fibre is one of five in this group*

*Fascicle is a bundle of muscle fibres bound by perimysium*

*Muscle wrapped by epimysium*

*Myofibril is one of many packed inside fibre*

◄ MUSCLE
Muscles consist mainly of muscle fibres, but also have blood vessels, nerve fibres, and connective tissue. This exploded view reveals the muscle fibres packed with myofibrils, which contain the filaments that produce contraction. Each muscle is surrounded by a protective, connective tissue sheath. Similar sheaths bind muscle fibres into bundles called fascicles. All these sheaths are continuous with the tendons that anchor muscles to bones, so when fibres contract, their full force acts on the bones they pull.

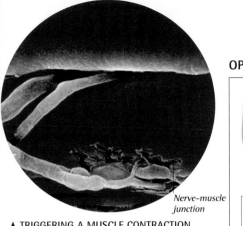

**▲ TRIGGERING A MUSCLE CONTRACTION**

Muscle contraction is triggered by electrical signals called nerve impulses. These arrive from the brain along nerve fibres, which branch into terminals (green), each serving its own muscle fibre (red). Nerve impulses pass into the muscle fibre where they activate the actin/myosin interaction that makes the muscle contract.

*Nerve-muscle junction*

## OPPOSING PAIRS OF MUSCLES

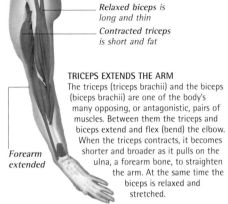

*Relaxed biceps is long and thin*
*Contracted triceps is short and fat*

**TRICEPS EXTENDS THE ARM**

The triceps (triceps brachii) and the biceps (biceps brachii) are one of the body's many opposing, or antagonistic, pairs of muscles. Between them the triceps and biceps extend and flex (bend) the elbow. When the triceps contracts, it becomes shorter and broader as it pulls on the ulna, a forearm bone, to straighten the arm. At the same time the biceps is relaxed and stretched.

*Forearm extended*

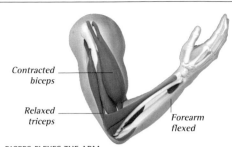

*Contracted biceps*
*Relaxed triceps*
*Forearm flexed*

**BICEPS FLEXES THE ARM**

The action of the biceps is opposite to that of the triceps. At one end, the biceps is joined to the shoulder bone (its origin), which does not move, and at the other end (its insertion), to a movable forearm bone called the radius. As with all muscles, when the biceps contracts, it pulls its insertion towards its fixed origin. As it bends the arm, the biceps gets shorter and fatter, while the relaxed triceps is long and narrow.

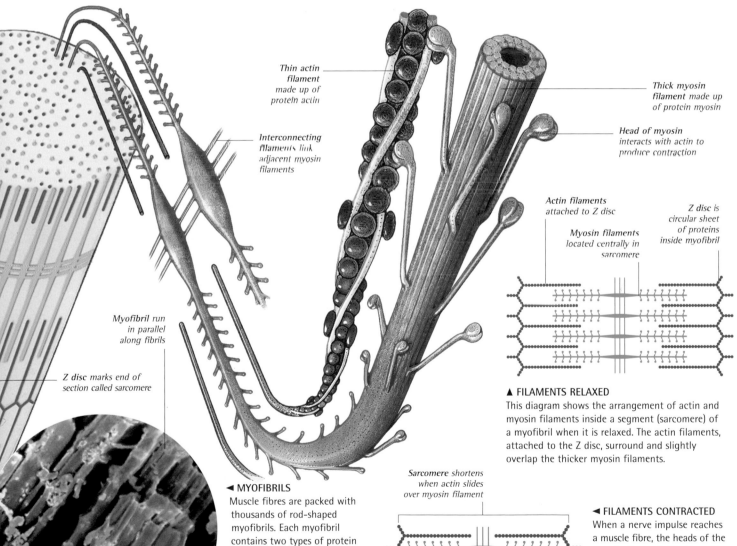

*Thin actin filament made up of protein actin*

*Interconnecting filaments link adjacent myosin filaments*

*Myofibril run in parallel along fibrils*

*Z disc marks end of section called sarcomere*

*Thick myosin filament made up of protein myosin*

*Head of myosin interacts with actin to produce contraction*

*Actin filaments attached to Z disc*
*Myosin filaments located centrally in sarcomere*
*Z disc is circular sheet of proteins inside myofibril*

**▲ FILAMENTS RELAXED**

This diagram shows the arrangement of actin and myosin filaments inside a segment (sarcomere) of a myofibril when it is relaxed. The actin filaments, attached to the Z disc, surround and slightly overlap the thicker myosin filaments.

**◄ MYOFIBRILS**

Muscle fibres are packed with thousands of rod-shaped myofibrils. Each myofibril contains two types of protein filament, called actin and myosin, which slide over each other to make the myofibril – and its muscle – contract. Filaments do not run the entire length of the myofibril. They are arranged in repeated patterns in segments called sarcomeres, and stretch between coin-like discs called Z discs.

*Sarcomere shortens when actin slides over myosin filament*

**◄ FILAMENTS CONTRACTED**

When a nerve impulse reaches a muscle fibre, the heads of the myosin filaments bind to actin filaments. Using energy, they swivel repeatedly towards the centre of the sarcomere, pulling in the actin filaments. The sarcomeres shorten, causing a muscle contraction, which persists until the impulses stop.

# MOVEMENT AND EXERCISE

The combination of different muscles, bones, and synovial (fully movable) joints in the body enable it to perform a wide range of movements. When we exercise, our muscles demand more oxygen and glucose to release extra energy, and the body responds by increasing heart and breathing rates. The ability of the body to respond efficiently depends on its fitness. Fitness includes stamina, strength, and flexibility – all of which are increased by regular exercise, although different types of exercise have particular benefits.

**▲ AEROBIC EXERCISE**

During all forms of aerobic exercise, such as swimming, fast walking, and running, muscles need extra oxygen to release energy in a process called aerobic respiration. The body responds by increasing heart and breathing rates. Taking aerobic exercise for 20 minutes, three times a week, significantly improves stamina. The heart becomes stronger, delivering nutrients and oxygen with much greater efficiency, and muscles develop an increased blood supply and more mitochondria, becoming more energy-efficient.

**BODY MOVEMENTS ►**

The dancer (right) is using a variety of movements as she performs. Bending and straightening her arms involves flexion, which bends a joint to bring bones closer together, and extension, which straightens a joint to move bones apart. Raising a leg or arm out to the side and down again uses abduction, which pulls a limb from the body's midline, and adduction, which pulls it back. Other movements include rotation, circumduction, and plantar flexion.

**ANAEROBIC EXERCISE ►**

Balancing on one hand, lifting weights, or sprinting over a short distance are all examples of anaerobic exercise. The muscles involved in such intensive, short-term exercises rapidly run out of oxygen, so have to switch to anaerobic (without oxygen) respiration to release energy. Anaerobic respiration is very efficient at providing energy for short periods but it creates an "oxygen debt" in the body, which must be "paid off" by extra breathing after exercise ceases.

exercise

*Arm and shoulder muscles have to work hard in this exercise to support the weight of the rest of the body in a fixed position*

*Circumduction moves entire limb in a circle*

*Rotation turns limb around its own long axis*

*Extension is a straightening movement*

*Plantar flexion bends the foot downwards*

*Dorsiflexion bends toes backwards*

*Adduction pulls the leg towards the body's midline*

*Abduction pulls the leg away from the body's midline*

| BENEFITS OF DIFFERENT EXERCISES | | | |
|---|---|---|---|
| *ACTIVITY* | *STRENGTH* | *STAMINA* | *FLEXIBILITY* |
| Swimming | ★★★★ | ★★★★★ | ★★★★ |
| Walking briskly | ★ | ★★ | ★ |
| Running | ★★ | ★★★★ | ★★ |
| Cycling fast | ★★★ | ★★★★ | ★★ |
| Dancing | ★ | ★★★ | ★★★★ |
| Yoga | ★ | ★ | ★★★★ |
| Basketball | ★★ | ★★★★ | ★★★ |
| Tennis | ★★ | ★★ | ★★★ |
| Climbing stairs | ★★★ | ★★★ | ★ |
| Watching TV | | | |

*Flexion is a
bending
movement*

## MONITORING EXERCISE

### WARM UP
A technician monitors a runner as she jogs slowly on a treadmill to "warm up" her muscles. Her breathing rate and oxygen usage are being measured, and she is wired to a monitor measuring her heart rate. Her heart rate (left scale – green line) and oxygen usage (right scale – blue line) are shown below.

### SUSTAINED EXERCISE
As the treadmill speed increases, and the runner runs at full speed, her heart rate more than doubles, and her oxygen usage almost doubles. Her heart also pumps out more blood with each beat; its output increases over fivefold to supply leg muscles with the extra oxygen they demand.

### RECOVERY
While the runner recovers, her heart rate and oxygen usage do not return to normal straight away. She still needs extra oxygen because some of her muscle energy was supplied by anaerobic respiration. The waste product of this process, lactic acid, needs to be disposed of by aerobic respiration.

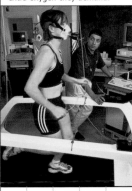

*(Graph: Heart rate (beats per minute) on left scale 60–160; Oxygen usage (litres per minute) on right scale 1–6; Time (minutes) on x-axis 0–35)*

## BLOOD FLOW TO BODY TISSUES

|  | | |
|---|---|---|
| HEART MUSCLE | 0.25 litres (½ pt) per min. | ■ BLOOD FLOW – AT REST |
| | 0.75 litres (1¼ pt) per min. | ■ BLOOD FLOW – EXERCISE |
| MUSCLE | 1.0 litres (1¾ pt) per min. | |
| | 12 litres (21 pt) per min. | |
| SKIN | 0.5 litres (1 pt) per min. | |
| | 2.0 litres (3½ pt) per min. | |
| DIGESTIVE SYSTEM | 1.5 litres (2¾ pt) per min. | |
| | 0.5 litres (1 pt) per min. | |

During exercise, the heart pumps out four to five times more blood than when the body is at rest. But body tissues do not share evenly in the increased blood flow, as this chart shows. Skeletal muscles receive a huge increase to supply them with extra energy. Heart muscle needs more blood to work faster, and skin needs extra to release heat. Meanwhile, blood flow to digestive organs decreases.

◄ FOOT PRESSURE
A baropedometer measures the pressure exerted by a foot during walking to produce a computer-generated, pressure distribution map like this one. The colours of the dots reveal areas of maximum pressure (dark blue), medium pressure (shades of light blue), and low pressure (white). This information can be used to tailor-make insoles for training shoes. These hold the feet and legs in position during exercise, reducing the risk of knee or back pain.

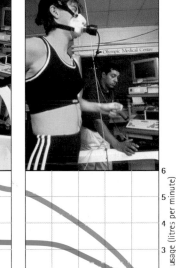

# OUTER COVERING

Wrapped around the body, skin provides a waterproof, germ-proof covering, which forms a barrier between the body's delicate inner tissues and the harsh world outside. Skin filters out harmful ultraviolet radiation in sunlight, helps the body maintain a steady temperature, and houses sensors that detect touch and pressure. It has two layers – the outer epidermis, from which hairs and nails grow, and the inner dermis. A range of micro-organisms live on the skin's surface.

**FINGERTIP**

Epidermal ridges aid gripping

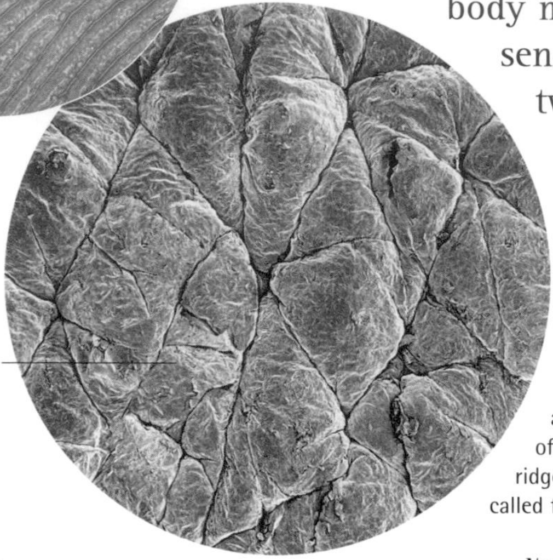

**SKIN ON LEG**

Bumps and grooves on the surface of the epidermis

**◄ SKIN**

Although skin appears to be smooth and flat, when viewed through a microscope or magnifying glass, it is covered by grooves and bumps. Its scaly skin flakes are continually worn away at the rate of tens of thousands per minute. The undersides of fingers and toes are covered by hundreds of curved epidermal ridges. These aid gripping and leave behind sweat patterns called fingerprints, which are unique to each individual.

**SKIN CROSS-SECTION ►**

A thin epidermis forms the outer part of the skin. At its surface is a scaly layer of dead, flattened cells packed with keratin, a tough, waterproofing protein. As these dead cells are worn away, they are replaced by constantly dividing, living cells in the basal layer. The dermis beneath is more complex. It has blood vessels, nerve fibres, sweat glands, and hair follicles – deep pits from which hairs grow. Sebaceous glands, attached to follicles, release oily sebum, which flows onto hairs and skin to keep them flexible and waterproof.

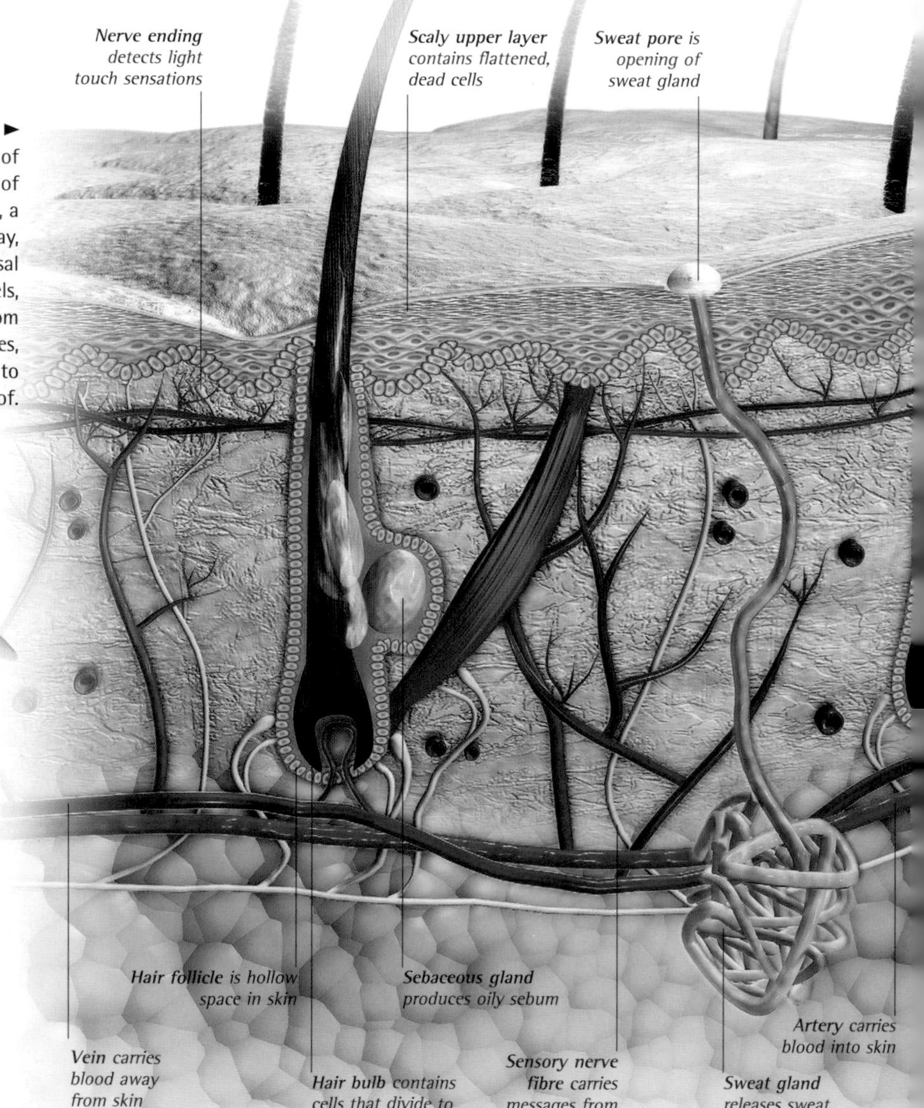

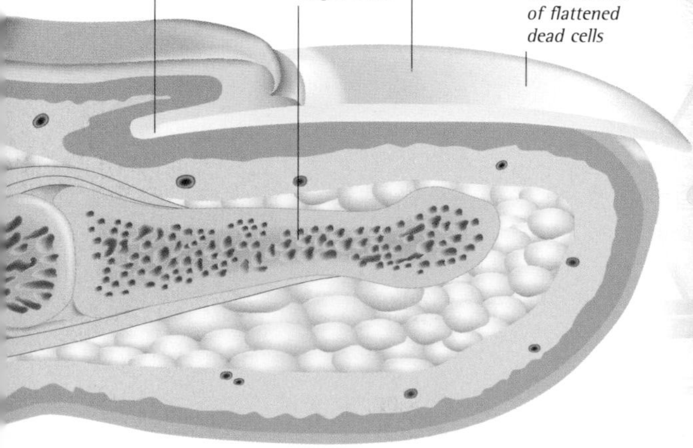

Nerve ending detects light touch sensations

Scaly upper layer contains flattened, dead cells

Sweat pore is opening of sweat gland

Nail root is embedded in skin

Phalanx is finger bone

Nail and finger shown in cross-section

Nail is made of flattened dead cells

**▲ NAIL**

Nails cover and protect the ends of fingers and toes and enable us to scratch and pick up small objects. They are hard, clear extensions of the epidermis and consist of flattened, dead cells, packed with tough keratin. They grow from living, constantly dividing cells in the nail root. Nails grow fastest in summer, and fingernails grow faster than toenails.

Hair follicle is hollow space in skin

Sebaceous gland produces oily sebum

Artery carries blood into skin

Vein carries blood away from skin

Hair bulb contains cells that divide to produce hair

Sensory nerve fibre carries messages from sensors

Sweat gland releases sweat onto skin surface

## ◄ HAIR

The body is covered by millions of hairs, each growing from a hair follicle. Cells at the base of the follicle divide to form the hair. As cells push upwards, they fill with keratin and die. The column of dead cells emerges from the follicle as the hair shaft. There are two types of hair. Fine, short hairs cover much of the body. Thicker hairs on the scalp protect it from the sun's effects and prevent heat loss, while eyelashes (left) protect the eyes.

*Hair shaft of eyelash grows out from follicle*

*Follicle mites protrude from a hair follicle*

*Sweat pore on skin's surface*

*Hair shaft grows out from follicle*

*Basal cell layer produces new epidermal cells*

*Epidermis is thin, outer part of skin*

*Dermis is thick, lower part of skin*

*Subcutaneous fat under skin insulates body*

*Arrector pili muscle pulls hair upright*

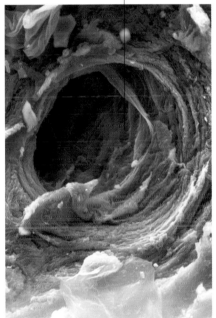

## ▲ SWEAT

Coiled sweat glands produce sweat, which they release through pores, like this one. Sweat is 99 per cent water with added salts and a little waste. It is filtered from blood that passes through the sweat gland. Sweat release is controlled by the nervous system. In hot conditions, the release of sweat onto the skin's surface increases. As the sweat evaporates, it cools the body by drawing heat from it, so helping to maintain a constant body temperature.

### SKIN, HAIR, AND NAIL FACTS AND FIGURES

| | |
|---|---|
| Skin mass | 5 kg (11 lb) |
| Skin surface area | 2 sq m (2½ sq yd) |
| Skin thickness (eyelid) | 0.5 mm |
| Skin thickness (sole of foot) | 4 mm (⅛ in) |
| Skin flakes lost per minute | 50,000 |
| Hairs on head | 100,000 |
| Hairs lost from head each day | 75–100 |
| Head hair growth (each month) | 10 mm (⅜ in) |
| Fingernail growth (summer month) | 5 mm (³⁄₁₆ in) |
| Toenail growth (summer month) | 1.5 mm (¹⁄₁₆ in) |
| Sweat pores per person | 2.5 million |

## ARTIFICIAL SKIN

A pair of forceps hold up a sheet of artificial skin (epidermis), which will be used to treat a patient who is suffering from burns to the skin. The tissue was produced by taking some of the patient's own epidermal cells while in the process of dividing, then growing them on a protein gel in a nutrient-rich culture solution. An epidermal sheet like this can be grown within a few weeks and then grafted onto sites where layers of skin have been destroyed.

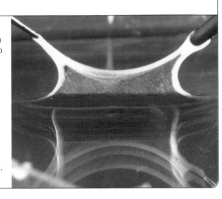

## ACNE ►

This rash of inflamed spots usually affects skin on the face, neck, shoulders, and back. Teenagers often develop acne because hormonal changes at puberty increase the secretion of oily sebum in some hair follicles. Blackheads form when excess sebum blocks follicles, hardens, and forms dark plugs. Whiteheads develop when excess keratin seals follicles, trapping a mass of white sebum inside. In both cases, bacteria infect the blocked sebum, causing inflammation and redness

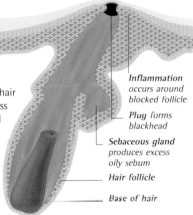

*Inflammation occurs around blocked follicle*

*Plug forms blackhead*

*Sebaceous gland produces excess oily sebum*

*Hair follicle*

*Base of hair*

## SKIN LIFE

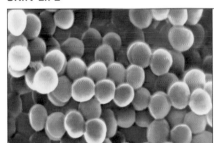

### BACTERIA

Each square centimetre of the skin is occupied by between 10,000 and one million micro-organisms, mainly bacteria (left). These microbes thrive in moist, warm conditions. Most bacteria that settle on the skin are harmless. They help keep skin healthy by forming a community that actively prevents harmful pathogens from living there.

### MITES

This is the front end of an eyelash mite (a sausage-shaped relative of the spider), which lives harmlessly in the eyelash follicles of most humans. Less pleasant is the itch or scabies mite. The female mite burrows under the skin to lay her eggs, causing severe itching. Scabies infections are treated using mite-killing lotions.

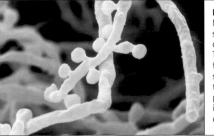

### FUNGUS

Most microscopic fungi on the skin are harmless, but some cause disease if they are allowed to thrive. This SEM shows filaments of a fungus that causes athlete's foot – sore, cracked, itchy skin between the toes. Wearing trainers for long periods can cause the problem, but it can be treated with antifungal drugs and improved foot hygiene.

# SENSITIVE SKIN

Skin is an important sense organ. It has a range of sensors that detect changes in touch, pressure, vibration, and temperature, as well as pain. Skin sensitivity varies according to the part of the body. Areas with numerous sensors, such as the fingertips, are highly sensitive, while those with fewer sensors, such as the back, are less sensitive. Epidermal cells in the skin produce a brown pigment called melanin, which filters harmful UV rays in sunlight. Exposure to sunlight increases melanin production and the skin's protection. The skin also plays a part in maintaining body temperature, under the control of the brain's hypothalamus.

*Free nerve ending responds to pain, heat, or cold*

*Epidermis is the upper layer of the skin*

## REGULATING BODY TEMPERATURE

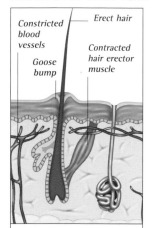

*Constricted blood vessels*
*Erect hair*
*Goose bump*
*Contracted hair erector muscle*

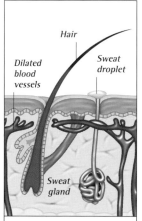

*Hair*
*Dilated blood vessels*
*Sweat droplet*
*Sweat gland*

### FEELING COLD
In cold conditions, blood vessels near the skin's surface constrict (narrow) to reduce heat loss from them. Hairs become erect and form goose bumps. Shivering may occur, releasing heat from muscles.

### FEELING HOT
In hot conditions, the skin is "instructed" to lose heat. Blood vessels near its surface dilate (widen), releasing heat like radiators. Sweat, released onto the skin's surface, evaporates and draws heat from the skin.

**SKIN RECEPTORS ▶**
The skin contains different types of skin receptors. Most – including Merkel's discs, Meissner's corpuscles, Pacinian corpuscles, and Ruffini's corpuscles – are mechanoreceptors that send nerve impulses to the brain or spinal cord when they are pressed or pulled. Meissner's corpuscles and Merkel's discs, both near the top of the dermis, detect light touch. Deeper Pacinian corpuscles detect pressure and vibration, while Ruffini's corpuscles respond to continuous touch. The free nerve endings are either nociceptors (pain detectors) or thermoreceptors (temperature sensors).

*Dermis is the lower, thicker layer of the skin*

skin

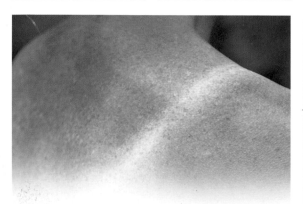

**▲ SUNBURN**
The amount of melanin, the protective pigment produced by the skin, increases with sensible exposure to sunlight, and darkens the skin. But sudden exposure of pale skin to sunlight, especially the midday sun in summer, can produce sunburn like this. The redness and soreness results from the damage caused to the outer layer of skin by UV rays. Repeated sunburn ages the skin more rapidly and increases the risk of developing skin cancer.

### MALIGNANT MELANOMA

This darkened, irregular patch on the skin is caused by malignant melanoma, a rare but serious form of skin cancer. Melanoma affect melanocytes, the cells in the epidermis that produce the brown pigment melanin, hence its colour. The major cause of malignant melanoma is over-exposure to intense sunlight, particularly in light-skinned people. Caught early, the growth can be removed surgically. However, if it is left untreated, melanoma spreads rapidly to other areas and may be fatal.

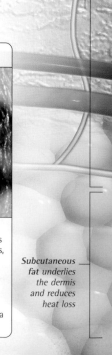

*Subcutaneous fat underlies the dermis and reduces heat loss*

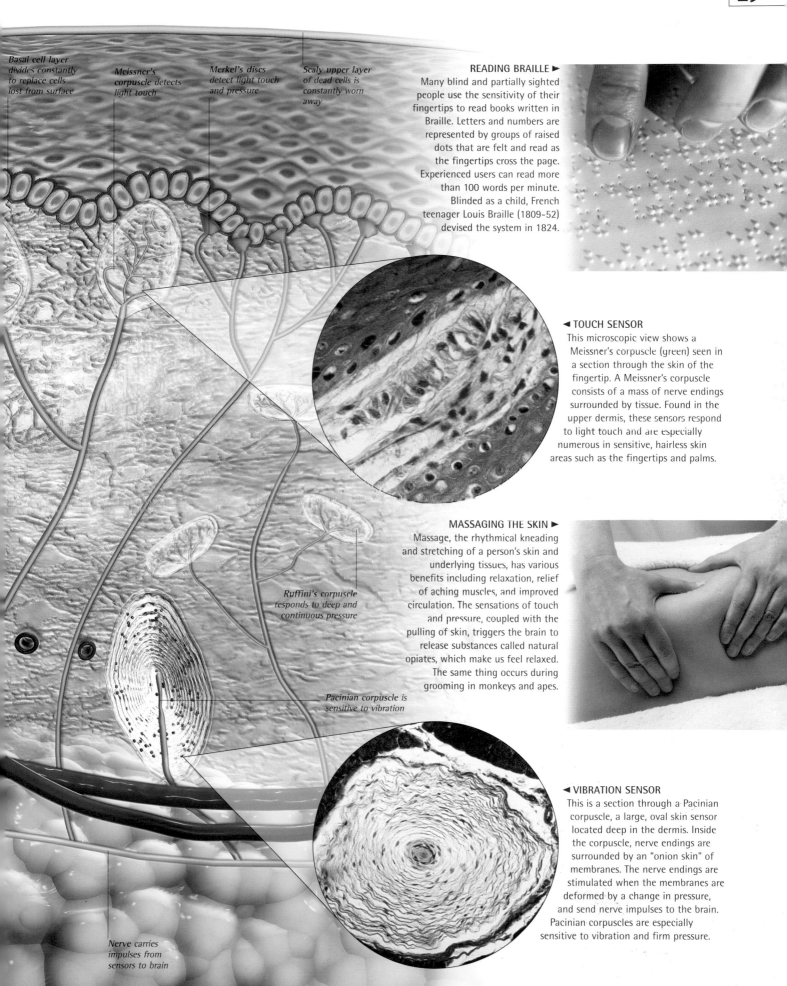

*Basal cell layer divides constantly to replace cells lost from surface*

*Meissner's corpuscle detects light touch*

*Merkel's discs detect light touch and pressure*

*Scaly upper layer of dead cells is constantly worn away*

### READING BRAILLE ▶

Many blind and partially sighted people use the sensitivity of their fingertips to read books written in Braille. Letters and numbers are represented by groups of raised dots that are felt and read as the fingertips cross the page. Experienced users can read more than 100 words per minute. Blinded as a child, French teenager Louis Braille (1809-52) devised the system in 1824.

### ◀ TOUCH SENSOR

This microscopic view shows a Meissner's corpuscle (green) seen in a section through the skin of the fingertip. A Meissner's corpuscle consists of a mass of nerve endings surrounded by tissue. Found in the upper dermis, these sensors respond to light touch and are especially numerous in sensitive, hairless skin areas such as the fingertips and palms.

*Ruffini's corpuscle responds to deep and continuous pressure*

### MASSAGING THE SKIN ▶

Massage, the rhythmical kneading and stretching of a person's skin and underlying tissues, has various benefits including relaxation, relief of aching muscles, and improved circulation. The sensations of touch and pressure, coupled with the pulling of skin, triggers the brain to release substances called natural opiates, which make us feel relaxed. The same thing occurs during grooming in monkeys and apes.

*Pacinian corpuscle is sensitive to vibration*

### ◀ VIBRATION SENSOR

This is a section through a Pacinian corpuscle, a large, oval skin sensor located deep in the dermis. Inside the corpuscle, nerve endings are surrounded by an "onion skin" of membranes. The nerve endings are stimulated when the membranes are deformed by a change in pressure, and send nerve impulses to the brain. Pacinian corpuscles are especially sensitive to vibration and firm pressure.

*Nerve carries impulses from sensors to brain*

# EYES AND VISION

Vision is the dominant sense, providing the brain with an immense amount of information about the body's surroundings. The sense organs responsible for vision are the eyes. They contain millions of photoreceptors, or light-sensitive cells, that respond to light from outside by sending nerve impulses to the brain. The brain interprets the nerve impulses as three-dimensional images that can be "seen". The eye has built-in systems that allow it to control the amount of light that enters it, and to focus light from objects on the retina, no matter how far away they are.

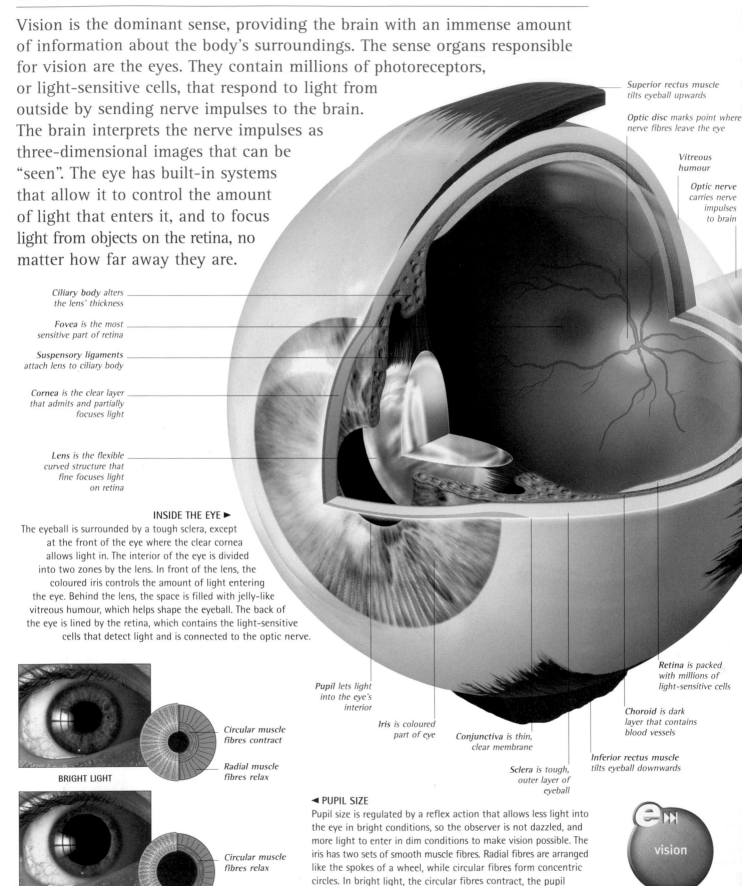

*Superior rectus muscle* tilts eyeball upwards

*Optic disc* marks point where nerve fibres leave the eye

*Vitreous humour*

*Optic nerve* carries nerve impulses to brain

*Ciliary body* alters the lens' thickness

*Fovea* is the most sensitive part of retina

*Suspensory ligaments* attach lens to ciliary body

*Cornea* is the clear layer that admits and partially focuses light

*Lens* is the flexible curved structure that fine focuses light on retina

### INSIDE THE EYE ▶
The eyeball is surrounded by a tough sclera, except at the front of the eye where the clear cornea allows light in. The interior of the eye is divided into two zones by the lens. In front of the lens, the coloured iris controls the amount of light entering the eye. Behind the lens, the space is filled with jelly-like vitreous humour, which helps shape the eyeball. The back of the eye is lined by the retina, which contains the light-sensitive cells that detect light and is connected to the optic nerve.

*Pupil* lets light into the eye's interior

*Iris* is coloured part of eye

*Conjunctiva* is thin, clear membrane

*Sclera* is tough, outer layer of eyeball

*Retina* is packed with millions of light-sensitive cells

*Choroid* is dark layer that contains blood vessels

*Inferior rectus muscle* tilts eyeball downwards

**BRIGHT LIGHT**

*Circular muscle fibres contract*

*Radial muscle fibres relax*

**DIM LIGHT**

*Circular muscle fibres relax*

*Radial muscle fibres contract*

### ◀ PUPIL SIZE
Pupil size is regulated by a reflex action that allows less light into the eye in bright conditions, so the observer is not dazzled, and more light to enter in dim conditions to make vision possible. The iris has two sets of smooth muscle fibres. Radial fibres are arranged like the spokes of a wheel, while circular fibres form concentric circles. In bright light, the circular fibres contract, the pupil constricts (narrows), and less light enters. In dim light, the radial fibres contract, the pupil dilates (widens), and more light enters.

vision

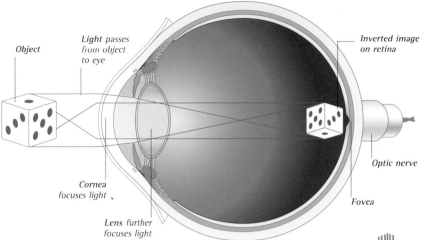

*Object* — *Light passes from object to eye* — *Inverted image on retina*

*Cornea focuses light* — *Lens further focuses light* — *Fovea* — *Optic nerve*

| VISION FACTS | |
| --- | --- |
| Mass of eyeball | 7 g (¼ oz) |
| Diameter of eyeball | 2.5 cm (1 in) |
| Percentage of body's sensory receptors in eyes | 70 per cent |
| Number of rods in each eye | 120 million |
| Number of cones in each eye | 6.5 million |
| Number of colours eyes can distinguish | 10,000 |
| Distance at which eyes can detect lighted candle | 1.6 km (1 mile) |

## ▲ FOCUSING AN IMAGE ON THE RETINA

Light rays are reflected from an object, in this case a die, into the eye. They are refracted (bent) first by the cornea and then by the lens. The resulting image, focused on the retina, is inverted (upside down). By looking directly at the object, light from it is focused on the fovea, the most sensitive part of the retina with a high concentration of cones. This will enable the brain to produce a clear, detailed image of the object.

## SENDING THE IMAGE TO THE BRAIN ▶

The retina is packed with photoreceptors (light-sensitive cells) called rods and cones. When light is focused on them, they generate nerve impulses, which are carried away by nerve cells and along the nerve fibres that form the optic nerve to the brain. Colour detection in bright light is provided by three types of cone that detect red, green, or blue light. The brain combines their input to produce a full-colour image.

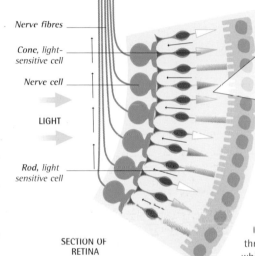

*Nerve fibres* — *Cone, light-sensitive cell* — *Nerve cell* — LIGHT — *Rod, light sensitive cell*

SECTION OF RETINA

## RODS AND CONES ▲

This SEM of a section through the retina shows rods and cones. Both convert light into electrical impulses, which travel to the brain. Around 120 million rods, which work best in dim light and cannot detect colours, are spread throughout the retina. Some 7 million cones, which provide detailed colour vision in bright light, are concentrated mainly in the fovea.

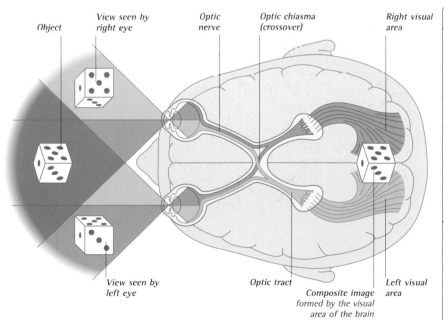

*Object* — *View seen by right eye* — *Optic nerve* — *Optic chiasma (crossover)* — *Right visual area*

*View seen by left eye* — *Optic tract* — *Composite image formed by the visual area of the brain* — *Left visual area*

## ▲ IMAGE FORMATION IN THE BRAIN

Nerve impulses travel along the optic nerves to the visual area at the rear of each cerebral hemisphere where they are reconstructed as the images, the right way up, that we "see". Nerve fibres run along the optic nerve to a point of crossover called the optic chiasma, where they partly cross, so signals from the right half of each eyeball pass to the right visual area, and those from the left half pass into the left visual area. By comparing differences in the input to the two areas, the brain can judge distances and see objects in three dimensions.

## CHANGING FOCUS

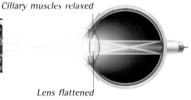

*Ciliary muscles relaxed*

DISTANT OBJECTS IN FOCUS — *Lens flattened*

### DISTANT VISION

The lens alters shape to fine focus light rays depending on whether they are from near or distant objects. Light rays from distant objects are nearly parallel, so need to be bent only a little by a flat lens to focus on the retina. The ciliary muscle around the lens relaxes, and fluid pressure inside the eyeball stretches the ring to pull the lens flat.

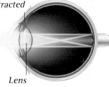

*Ciliary muscles contracted*

NEARBY OBJECT IN FOCUS — *Lens rounded*

### NEAR VISION

Light rays from near objects are diverging (spreading apart) as they enter the eye. The lens becomes thicker and more curved to bend these light rays and focus them on the retina. The ring of ciliary muscle contracts and stops pulling on the lens, which reverts to its normal round shape.

# HEARING AND BALANCE

Ears are sense organs that lie mostly concealed within the skull. They detect sounds and also help the body maintain balance and posture. Each ear has an outer, middle, and inner section. Sound waves entering the ear are detected by sound sensors in the inner ear. These send nerve signals to the brain, which are interpreted as sounds. Balance receptors in the inner ear detect the position and movement of the body. This information, combined with input from sensors in muscles, joints, and the eyes, enables us to keep upright and balanced.

**senses**

**◄ EAR OSSICLES**
These three tiny bones, which stretch across the air-filled middle ear, are called the hammer, anvil, and stirrup. The hammer is attached to the eardrum, while the stirrup is attached to the oval window, a membrane covering the entrance to the inner ear. When sound waves make the eardrum vibrate, the ossicles transmit the vibrations to the inner ear.

**EAR STRUCTURE ►**
The outer ear consists of the pinna, which directs sound waves into the ear, and the 2.5-cm (1-in) long, air-filled outer ear canal, which carries sounds to the eardrum. Wax released by wax glands cleans the ear canal and deters insects. The middle ear, also air-filled, is straddled by the three ossicles. The inner ear contains fluid-filled channels. The "hearing" part of the ear is the cochlea. The vestibular complex is involved in maintaining balance.

*Vestibular nerve*   *Cochlear nerve*

*Vestibular complex helps maintain balance*

**EARDRUM ►**
Taut as a drumskin, the eardrum, or tympanic membrane, seals the inner end of the outer ear canal and separates it from the middle ear. It is made from a translucent, connective tissue membrane (right). When sound waves travelling along the ear canal finally reach the eardrum, it vibrates and passes on the sound energy to the ossicles in the middle ear.

*Wax gland produces earwax*

*Ossicles cross middle ear*

*Cochlea in inner ear detects sounds*

*Eardrum divides outer and middle ears*

*Eustachian tube equalizes air pressure*

*Outer ear canal carries sound waves from outside*

*Sensory hairs*

*Hair cell*

**▼ PASSAGE OF SOUND**
Sound waves hitting the eardrum make it vibrate, causing the three linked ossicles to move like a piston, pushing the oval window in and out. This creates vibrations in the fluid filling the coiled passageways of the cochlea, which distort the hair cells within the organ of Corti. The hair cells send nerve impulses along the cochlear nerve to the auditory (hearing) area of the brain, where they are interpreted as sounds.

*Hammer (malleus)*   *Stirrup (stapes)*   *Path of incoming vibration*

*Anvil (incus)*

*Cochlear nerve*

*Organ of Corti*

*Hair cells*

*Nerve fibres*

*Nerve impulse travelling to cochlear nerve*

*Vibrations tweak "hairs" of hair cells*

*Outer ear canal*   *Oval window*

*Eardrum*

**HAIR CELLS ▲**
Up to 15,000 hair cells in the organ of Corti within the cochlea convert sound vibrations into nerve impulses. The long, thin cells have a V-shaped tuft of "hairs" projecting from the top of them. Sound vibrations rippling through the fluid filling the cochlea bend the hairs. This makes the hair cells generate nerve impulses that travel to the brain.

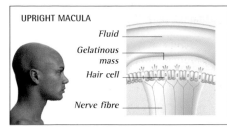

## SENSING GRAVITY AND ACCELERATION

### UPRIGHT MACULA

Fluid
Gelatinous mass
Hair cell
Nerve fibre

### HORIZONTAL
Here the macula of utricle is in its upright, horizontal position. The macula consists of sensitive hair cells embedded in a gelatinous mass that carries otoliths, crystals of calcium carbonate (chalk). Nerve fibres from the hair cells enter the vestibular nerve.

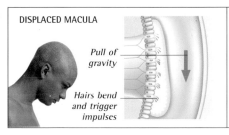

### DISPLACED MACULA

Pull of gravity
Hairs bend and trigger impulses

### TILTING OR ACCELERATING
When the head tilts forwards, the weight of the otoliths makes the macula slide downwards under gravity. This triggers hair cells to send signals to the brain. Horizontal movements produce the same effect. The saccule is affected by vertical movement, such as going up in a lift.

## SENSING TURNING MOVEMENT

### STABLE CUPULA

Fluid
Cupula
Hair cell
Nerve fibre

### STATIONARY
The three semicircular canals work together to detect speed and direction of the rotation of the head. At the base of each canal is a swelling called the ampulla that contains a jelly-like cupula – shown here in a stationary position – in which are embedded hair cells.

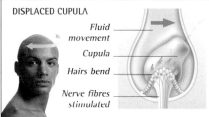

### DISPLACED CUPULA

Fluid movement
Cupula
Hairs bend
Nerve fibres stimulated

### TURNING
When the head turns, fluid in the semicircular canal moves in the opposite direction, causing the cupula to bend. This stimulates hair cells to send nerve impulses to the brain. The canals, being at right angles, can detect rotatory movement in any direction.

---

Semicircular canal is one of three

Fluid-filled duct within semicircular canal

Vestibular nerve carries signals from balance organs to brain

Ampulla contains cupula

Cupula contains sensory hair cells

Utricle detects horizontal and tilting movements

Macula of utricle is horizontal

Macula of saccule is vertical

Saccule detects vertical movements

### BALANCE ORGANS ▲
There are two sets of fluid-filled balance organs in the inner ear. They send nerve impulses that update the brain about the body's position and movement, so helping it to maintain balance and posture. The utricle and saccule contain hair cells that detect linear (straight line) acceleration and deceleration and the position of the head when it is not moving. The three semicircular canals, set at right angles to each other, detect head rotation in any direction.

### FREQUENCY

A sound's frequency is the speed at which sound makes the air vibrate. High frequency sounds are high-pitched; low frequency sounds are low-pitched. Young people hear sounds in the range 20 Hz to 20,000 Hz, but the upper limit declines with age. Other animals have different frequency ranges.

| ANIMAL | MIN. FREQUENCY (HERTZ) | MAX. FREQUENCY (HERTZ) |
|---|---|---|
| Human (10-year-old) | 20 | 20,000 |
| Human (60-year-old) | 20 | 12,000 |
| Goldfish | 20 | 3,000 |
| Dog | 60 | 45,000 |
| Frog | 100 | 3,000 |
| Cat | 60 | 65,000 |
| Porpoise | 75 | 150,000 |
| Bat | 1,000 | 120,000 |

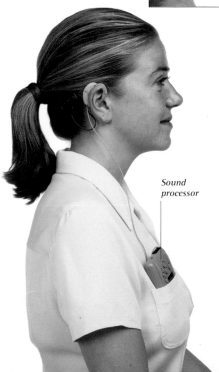

Sound processor

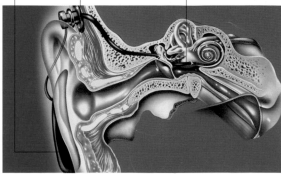

Microphone
Transmitter
Electrical wire contacts cochlear nerve here

### ◄ COCHLEAR IMPLANT
A cochlear implant can, in some cases, help people who are profoundly deaf. A tiny wire is implanted surgically in the cochlea along with a receiver in the skull above the ear. A microphone detects sounds that pass to the sound processor, which sends signals via the transmitter to the wire in the cochlea. This stimulates the cochlear nerve and sends impulses to the brain, enabling sound patterns to be detected.

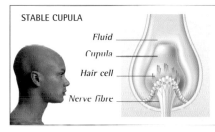

# TASTE AND SMELL

Taste and smell are linked senses because they both depend on sensors, called chemoreceptors, which detect chemicals dissolved in water. Smell is about 10,000 times more sensitive than taste. Together smell and taste allow us to detect and appreciate flavours, and identify odours such as smoke, or tastes such as bitter poisons, which might be dangerous and need to be avoided. These senses vary widely in people, which is why food or wine tasters can make a career out of their extra sensitivity to tastes and smells.

senses

**NOSE AND MOUTH ▶**
Smell, or olfactory, receptors are found in the nasal cavity. When triggered by odours, they send nerve impulses primarily to the limbic system, an area of the brain involved with emotion and memory. This explains why certain smells evoke a strong emotional response. Taste receptors are found on the surface of the tongue and send nerve signals through two cranial nerves to the taste areas of the cerebrum.

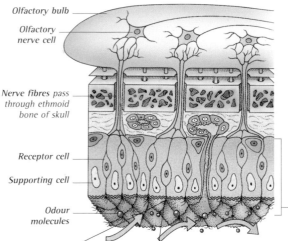

Olfactory bulb
Olfactory nerve cell
Nerve fibres pass through ethmoid bone of skull
Receptor cell
Supporting cell
Odour molecules

Olfactory bulb carries nerve impulses to brain
Olfactory nerve fibres carry signals from smell receptors
Olfactory epithelium
Nasal cavity
Nose
Epithelium

Left cerebral hemisphere
Olfactory pathway to limbic system

Mouth

**▲ SMELL DETECTION**
Smell receptors are found high in the nasal cavity in a patch of tissue called the olfactory (smell) epithelium. When these receptor cells detect odour molecules in the air, they send signals along the nerve fibres that pass through holes in the ethmoid bone of the skull, which forms the top of the nasal cavity. These signals are then relayed along the olfactory bulb to the brain.

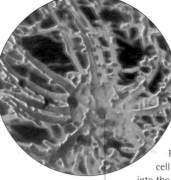

**◀ OLFACTORY CILIA**
Projecting from the end of each olfactory receptor cell are 10 to 20 hair-like cilia. When air is breathed into the nasal cavity, odour molecules dissolve in the watery mucus that covers the olfactory epithelium and cilia. The cilia carry a range of sites, each of which binds to specific odours. When odour molecules bind to the sites, the receptor cell sends nerve impulses to the brain. This allows us to experience and distinguish between the smell of a rose and that of a bonfire.

Olfactory receptor with a mass of cilia

Tongue surface contains taste sensors

Cranial nerves carry signals from tongue

## TASTING BY PROFESSION

Some people with an inherited heightened sense of smell and taste use it to make a living as, perhaps, a tea or wine taster or a perfumier. Their inherited ability can be trained and refined to enable them to detect subtle differences in flavour and scent.

This wine taster is assessing a wine in terms of its bouquet (odour), taste, and the combination of both in its flavour. Words that are often used to describe wine, such as "woody" or "lemony", reflect this combination of scent and taste. The wine taster also uses vision to assess the wine's colour and clarity.

*Pathways followed by nerve signals from tongue to taste centre in left cerebral hemisphere*

### TONGUE TASTE MAP ▶
The taste sensations that we experience can be grouped into one of four basic taste qualities – sweet, salty, sour, and bitter. Different parts of the tongue are sensitive to different tastes, even though there is no obvious difference in taste buds in different areas of the tongue. The tip is most sensitive to sweet and salty tastes, the sides to sour tastes, and the rear to bitter tastes – a pattern shown in a taste map like this one.

*Epiglottis at back of throat*

*Bitter tastes detected here*

*Sour tastes detected here*

*Salty tastes detected here*

*Sweet tastes detected here*

### ▼ SURFACE OF THE TONGUE
The surface of the tongue is covered by tiny projections called papillae, seen here much magnified. There are two main types. Mushroom-like fungiform papillae house taste buds, mainly around their edges. Spiky filiform papillae lack taste buds, but grip food during chewing. They also have sensors that help us detect the texture and temperature of food – to distinguish, for example, between a hot potato and cold ice cream. They also enable us to detect pain.

### TASTE AND SMELL FACT FILE

| | |
|---|---|
| Number of taste buds | 10,000 |
| Number of olfactory receptors | millions |
| Tastes detected by the tongue | 4 |
| Number of smells detected by human nose | 10,000 |
| Area of olfactory epithelium | 5 sq cm ($^3/_4$ sq in) |
| Lowest odour concentration detectable (methyl mercaptan – added to natural gas to make it smell) | 1 part in 25 billion |
| Number of genes controlling sense of smell | 1,000 |

*Filiform papilla detects texture and temperature*

*Fungiform papilla houses taste buds*

*Taste pore is opening of taste bud*

*Surface cell of tongue*

*Taste hair detects dissolved substances in saliva*

*Receptor cell sends nerve signals when tastes detected*

*Supporting cell supports taste cells*

*Nerve fibre carries nerve signal to brain*

### TASTE BUD ▶
Each taste bud consists of sensory and supporting cells, which are grouped together like the segments of an orange beneath a taste pore. During chewing, chemicals in food and drink dissolve in saliva, enter the taste pore, and are detected by taste hairs projecting from the sensory cells. The cells then generate nerve impulses, which are sent to the brain's taste centre and supply a taste experience.

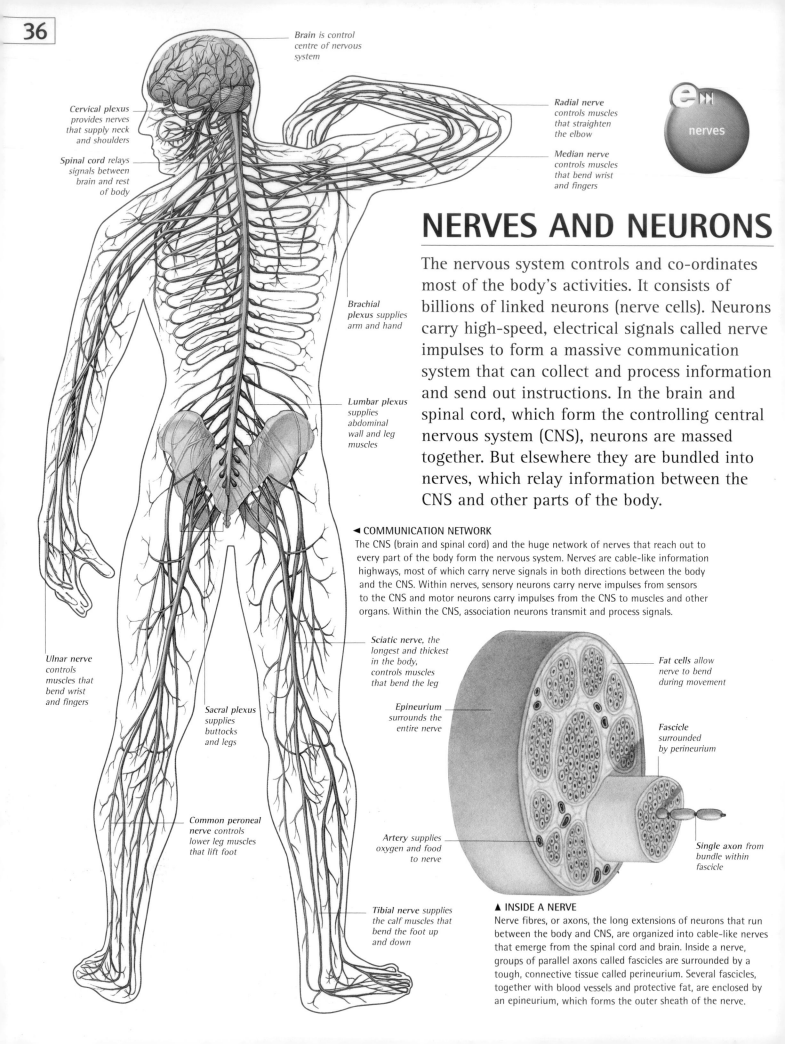

Brain is control centre of nervous system

Cervical plexus provides nerves that supply neck and shoulders

Spinal cord relays signals between brain and rest of body

Radial nerve controls muscles that straighten the elbow

Median nerve controls muscles that bend wrist and fingers

nerves

Brachial plexus supplies arm and hand

Lumbar plexus supplies abdominal wall and leg muscles

Ulnar nerve controls muscles that bend wrist and fingers

Sacral plexus supplies buttocks and legs

Common peroneal nerve controls lower leg muscles that lift foot

Sciatic nerve, the longest and thickest in the body, controls muscles that bend the leg

Epineurium surrounds the entire nerve

Artery supplies oxygen and food to nerve

Tibial nerve supplies the calf muscles that bend the foot up and down

Fat cells allow nerve to bend during movement

Fascicle surrounded by perineurium

Single axon from bundle within fascicle

# NERVES AND NEURONS

The nervous system controls and co-ordinates most of the body's activities. It consists of billions of linked neurons (nerve cells). Neurons carry high-speed, electrical signals called nerve impulses to form a massive communication system that can collect and process information and send out instructions. In the brain and spinal cord, which form the controlling central nervous system (CNS), neurons are massed together. But elsewhere they are bundled into nerves, which relay information between the CNS and other parts of the body.

◀ COMMUNICATION NETWORK

The CNS (brain and spinal cord) and the huge network of nerves that reach out to every part of the body form the nervous system. Nerves are cable-like information highways, most of which carry nerve signals in both directions between the body and the CNS. Within nerves, sensory neurons carry nerve impulses from sensors to the CNS and motor neurons carry impulses from the CNS to muscles and other organs. Within the CNS, association neurons transmit and process signals.

▲ INSIDE A NERVE

Nerve fibres, or axons, the long extensions of neurons that run between the body and CNS, are organized into cable-like nerves that emerge from the spinal cord and brain. Inside a nerve, groups of parallel axons called fascicles are surrounded by a tough, connective tissue called perineurium. Several fascicles, together with blood vessels and protective fat, are enclosed by an epineurium, which forms the outer sheath of the nerve.

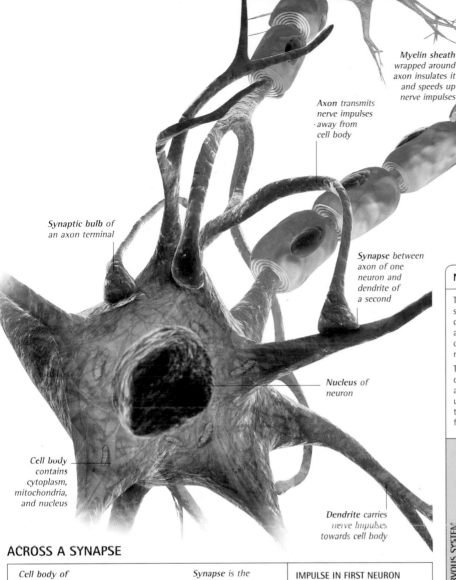

*Myelin sheath wrapped around axon insulates it and speeds up nerve impulses*

*Axon transmits nerve impulses away from cell body*

*Gap between myelin sheaths allow nerve impulses to leapfrog along axon*

*Synaptic bulb of an axon terminal*

*Synapse between axon of one neuron and dendrite of a second*

*Nucleus of neuron*

*Cell body contains cytoplasm, mitochondria, and nucleus*

*Dendrite carries nerve impulses towards cell body*

## ◄ NEURON

Each neuron has a cell body containing the nucleus, short filaments called dendrites that carry impulses to the cell body, and a long fine filament (the axon or nerve fibre) which carries nerve impulses to the next neuron. The axon of many neurons is surrounded by a fatty myelin sheath that insulates the axon and speeds up the movement of nerve impulses up to 100 m/s (328 ft/s). Each neuron is in contact with many others.

## NERVOUS SYSTEM

The nervous system is split into the CNS and the peripheral nervous system (PNS). The CNS – the brain and spinal cord – co-ordinates and controls the body's activities by processing input from sense organs and sending out instructions to muscles and other organs. The PNS consists of the nerves that extend from the brain and spinal cord and relay nerve impulses between the CNS and the rest of the body.

The PNS has sensory, somatic, and autonomic divisions. The sensory division gathers information about changes inside and outside the body and sends it to the CNS along sensory neurons. The somatic division is under conscious control and carries instructions via motor neurons from the brain to skeletal muscles. The autonomic division relays instructions from the CNS to control the activities of internal organs automatically.

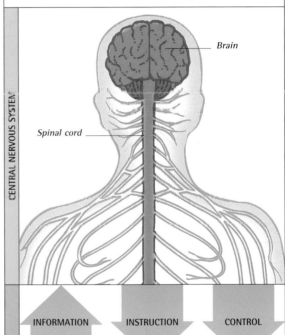

*Brain*

*Spinal cord*

**CENTRAL NERVOUS SYSTEM**

**PERIPHERAL NERVOUS SYSTEM**

INFORMATION | INSTRUCTION | CONTROL

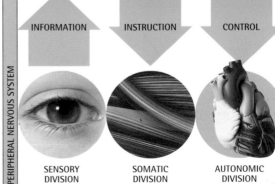

**SENSORY DIVISION** | **SOMATIC DIVISION** | **AUTONOMIC DIVISION**

*The sensory division informs the CNS of external changes detected by the senses and internal changes, such as having a full bladder.* | *The somatic division sends the instructions that enable conscious movement of different muscles to, for example, wave a hand or kick a ball.* | *The workings of internal organs, such as heart and breathing rates, are controlled automatically by the autonomic division.*

## ACROSS A SYNAPSE

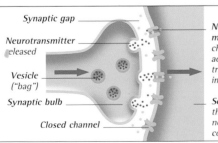

*Cell body of first neuron* — *Axon* — *Synapse is the junction between one neuron and the next*

*Nerve impulse travels along axon of first neuron towards adjacent neuron* — *Myelin sheath* — *Dendrite*

### IMPULSE IN FIRST NEURON
Neurons meet at junctions called synapses, where they are separated by a small gap. A nerve impulse travels at high speed along the axon of a neuron. At the end of this neuron, an axon terminal makes contact with the dendrite of an adjacent neuron at the synapse. The impulse is transmitted across the gap in chemical not electrical form.

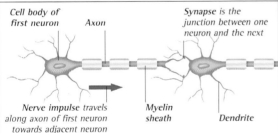

*Synaptic gap* — *Neurotransmitter released* — *Vesicle ("bag")* — *Synaptic bulb* — *Closed channel*

*Neurotransmitter opens channel to admit ions that trigger nerve impulses*

*Second neuron through which nerve impulse continues*

### CHEMICAL TRANSFER
At the end of the axon terminal is the synaptic bulb, containing vesicles of neurotransmitter (red), the chemical that transfers the nerve impulse across the synaptic gap. When the nerve impulse reaches the bulb, vesicles release neurotransmitter molecules into the gap and trigger a nerve impulse in the second neuron.

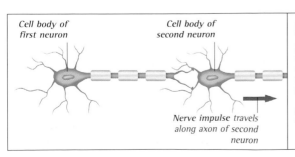

*Cell body of first neuron* — *Cell body of second neuron*

*Nerve impulse travels along axon of second neuron*

### IMPULSE IN SECOND NEURON
The newly generated impulse passes along the axon of the second neuron. Any remaining neurotransmitter in the synaptic gap is broken down by enzymes so that the second neuron does not fire repeatedly without stimulation. Impulses cannot be transmitted chemically in the reverse direction across a synapse.

# SPINAL CORD

The spinal cord is a column of nervous tissue that extends from the base of the brain down through the back. It plays an important part in controlling the body and processing information by acting as an information highway relaying signals between the brain and the body. The spinal cord also controls many of the body's reflex actions. These are rapid responses that occur without conscious intervention and often protect the body from danger.

**SPINAL CORD AND NERVES ▶**
No wider than a finger, the spinal cord extends down the back from the base of the brain to the lumbar vertebrae. Thirty-one pairs of spinal nerves spread out to control most of the body's skeletal muscles and to carry incoming messages from sensors around the body, including the skin.

spinal cord

*Cerebrum* is the conscious part of the brain

*Cerebellum* is the section of the brain controlling movement

*Brain stem* links the brain to the spinal cord

*Spinal cord* runs from the brain down the back

*Paired spinal nerves* attached to spinal cord

## SCANNING FOR DAMAGE

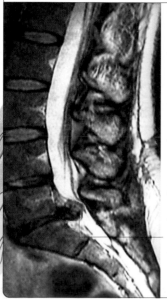

The intervertebral discs between adjacent vertebrae act as slightly movable joints and as shock absorbers between the bones. Each disc consists of a tough fibrous coat with a jelly-like centre. As seen in this MRI scan of the lower backbone, the fibrous coat sometimes ruptures or breaks open. The jelly-like core (blue) protrudes and puts pressure on spinal tissue (white), often causing back pain and weakness in the legs. This is called a disc prolapse or, more usually, a slipped disc.

*Slipped disc* pressing on nervous tissue in spine

*Lumbar spinal nerves* supply the lower back and legs

*Sacral spinal nerves* supply the buttocks, legs, feet, and genital areas

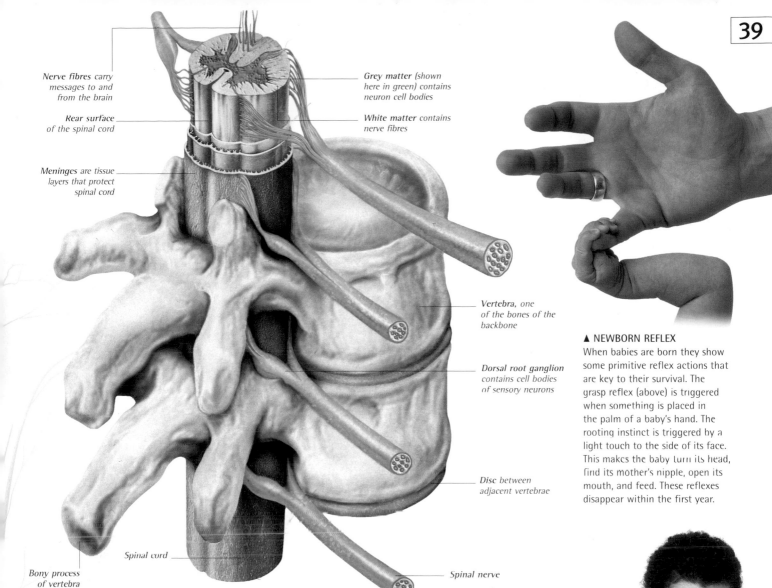

Nerve fibres carry messages to and from the brain

Rear surface of the spinal cord

Meninges are tissue layers that protect spinal cord

Grey matter (shown here in green) contains neuron cell bodies

White matter contains nerve fibres

Vertebra, one of the bones of the backbone

Dorsal root ganglion contains cell bodies of sensory neurons

Disc between adjacent vertebrae

Spinal cord

Spinal nerve

Bony process of vertebra

## ▲ SPINAL CORD STRUCTURE

The spinal cord is protected by a "tunnel", formed from bony arches of vertebrae, and by three connective tissue layers called meninges. In the centre of the spinal cord is grey matter, surrounded by white matter. The grey matter relays signals between the sensory and motor neurons (see p.36), while the white matter contains nerve fibres that carry signals to and from the brain. Spinal nerves emerge between neighbouring vertebrae.

## ▲ NEWBORN REFLEX

When babies are born they show some primitive reflex actions that are key to their survival. The grasp reflex (above) is triggered when something is placed in the palm of a baby's hand. The rooting instinct is triggered by a light touch to the side of its face. This makes the baby turn its head, find its mother's nipple, open its mouth, and feed. These reflexes disappear within the first year.

Hands cover the eyes for protection

## PAIN REACTIONS

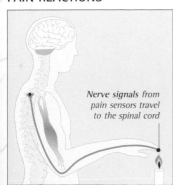

Nerve signals from pain sensors travel to the spinal cord

### HARMFUL STIMULUS

The withdrawal reflex is an automatic self-protecting response triggered when something sharp or hot is touched. Pain receptors in the skin of the fingertips detect the burning stimulus of the candle flame and send nerve impulses along sensory neurons to the spinal cord. Impulses are relayed at high speed across the spinal cord by association neurons.

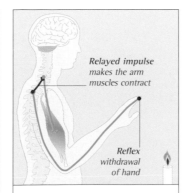

Relayed impulse makes the arm muscles contract

Reflex withdrawal of hand

### AUTOMATIC WITHDRAWAL

Within milliseconds (thousandths of a second) of the painful stimulus being detected, nerve impulses have been passed on to motor neurons. These neurons relay them to flexor (bending) muscles in the upper arm. On receiving the impulses, these muscles contract, bending the arm and pulling the fingers away from the flame before much harm is caused.

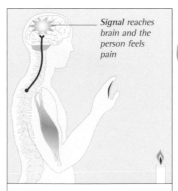

Signal reaches brain and the person feels pain

### FEELING PAIN

Nerve fibres in the spinal cord carry nerve impulses to the sensory areas of the brain where, at last, pain is felt. This only occurs after the reflex withdrawal has taken place. The time taken for impulses to travel along a reflex arc – the pathway involved in a reflex – is much shorter than the time taken to reach the brain.

### SELF PROTECTION ▲

Some reflexes are processed by the brain instead of the spinal cord. For example, three levels of reflex protect the eyes. A minor threat, such as an insect, causes us to blink to protect the eyes. Something potentially more damaging, such as a fast-moving object, causes the head to pull back automatically. At the highest level of risk – for example, a chemical sprayed at the face – we lift our hands to shield our face.

# CONTROL CENTRE

The brain is the control centre of the nervous system and consists of more than 100 billion interlinked neurons. The main part of the brain, the cerebrum, processes and sends out nerve signals, enabling us to experience the world around us, to move in a co-ordinated way, and to think, create, learn, and be self-aware. The brain's two halves – the left and right cerebral hemispheres – each control their opposite side of the body. Other brain areas are responsible for the automatic control of body functions such as breathing, blinking, and the the strength and rate of the heartbeat.

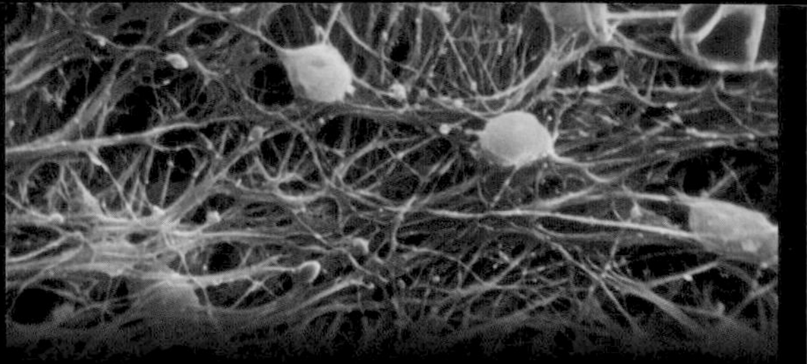

**BRAIN NEURONS ▲**
These are just a few of the billions of neurons that form the brain's vast communication and information processing system. Each neuron forms links with hundreds or even thousands of other neurons through more than one trillion synapses (relay spaces between neurons) to provide a massive network of pathways.

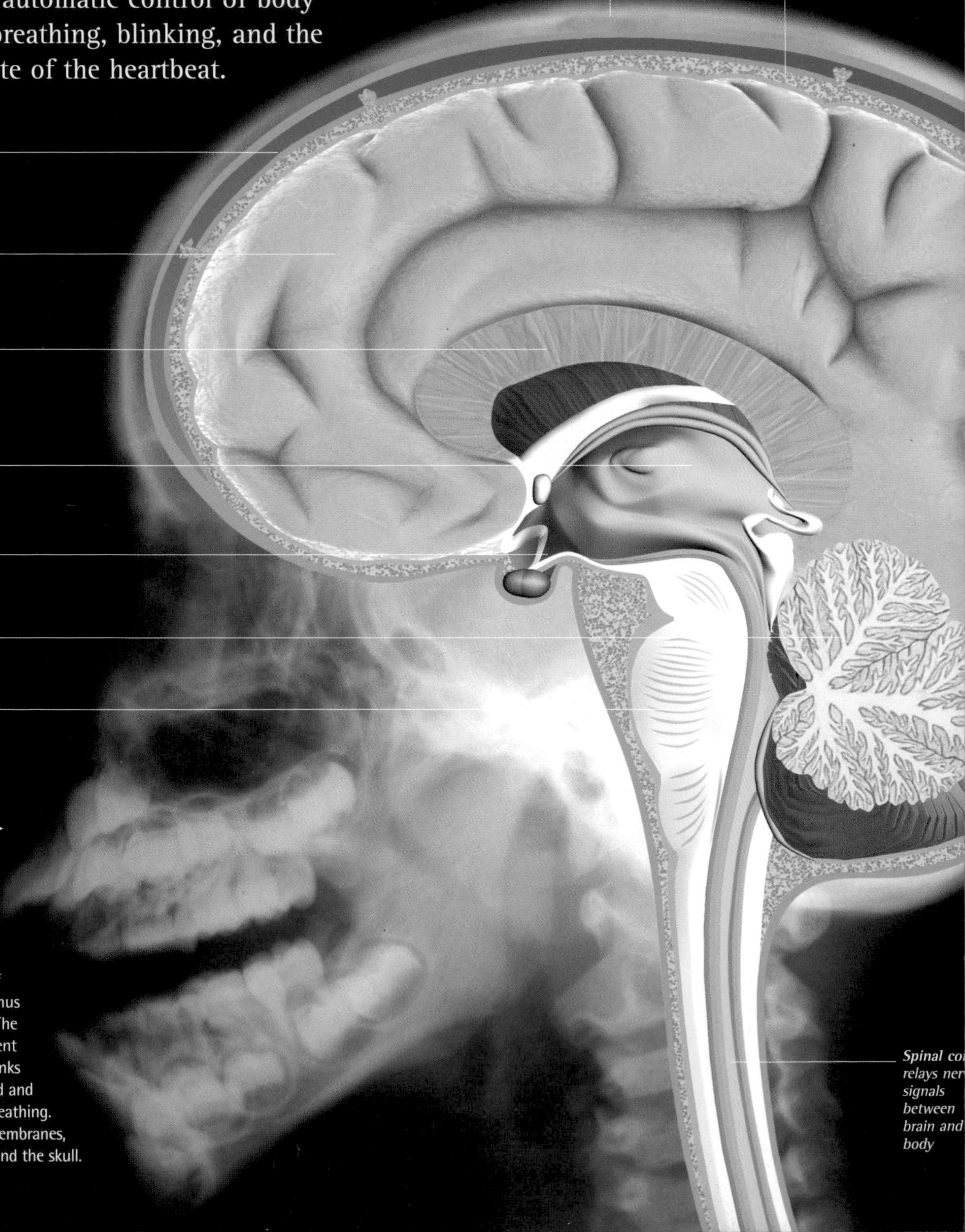

**Skull** forms hard, protective casing

**Subarachnoid space** between two inner meninges contains shock-absorbing fluid

**Sagittal vein** runs around the top of brain and removes oxygen-poor blood

**Right hemisphere of cerebrum** controls left side of body

**Corpus callosum** links left and right cerebral hemispheres

**Thalamus** relays sensory signals from body to cerebrum

**Hypothalamus** regulates sleep, hunger, and body temperature

**Cerebellum** controls body movements

**Brain stem** controls vital functions such as breathing and heart rate

**INSIDE THE BRAIN ▶**
The brain, seen here in vertical section, has three main regions – the forebrain, cerebellum, and brain stem. The forebrain consists of the cerebrum's two hemispheres, which make up 85 per cent of the brain's mass, and the thalamus and hypothalamus below it. The cerebellum co-ordinates movement and balance. The brain stem links the cerebrum to the spinal cord and controls life processes such as breathing. The brain is protected by three membranes, called meninges, and the skull.

**Spinal co** relays ner signals between brain and body

Prefrontal cortex (A) is
involved in reasoning
and planning

Premotor cortex (A)
co-ordinates complex
movements

Broca's area (M)
produces speech

Primary auditory
cortex (S) receives
input from ears

Auditory association
cortex (A)
interprets sounds

Motor cortex (M)
instructs muscles
to contract

Primary sensory cortex
(S) receives signals
from skin sensors

Sensory association
cortex (A) interprets
skin sensations

Visual association
cortex (A) forms
"images"

Primary visual
cortex (S) receives
input from eyes

**BRAIN MAP ▶**
The thin outer layer of each
hemisphere, the cerebral cortex,
processes and stores information,
and initiates body movements. Distinct
areas of the cortex carry out specific tasks,
as this brain map of the left hemisphere shows, but
none operate in isolation. Sensory areas (S) receive input
from sensors in, for example, the skin. Motor areas (M) send
instructions to muscles. About 75 per cent of the cortex
consists of association areas (A). These interpret and analyse
information and enable us to learn, plan, and be self-aware.

## HOW A STROKE DAMAGES THE BRAIN

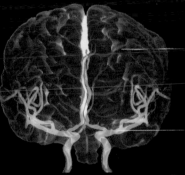

Normal brain tissue

Healthy arteries
supply brain with
oxygen-rich blood

Right cerebral
hemisphere works
normally

Blood escapes
from burst artery
in left cerebral
hemisphere

These MRA scans show front views of the brain and the arteries that
supply it. The brain uses up to one-fifth of the body's oxygen intake,
and brain neurons die rapidly if their supply is interrupted. The top scan
shows healthy arteries supplying both left and right hemispheres with
oxygen-rich blood. The lower scan shows the brain of someone who has
suffered a stroke. An artery supplying the left cerebral hemisphere has
burst, causing bleeding, and neurons in the area are deprived of oxygen
and die. This can result in a person becoming, for example, paralysed on
the right side of the body. Strokes are also caused by blockages in arteries.

## FROM BRAIN TO FINGER AND BACK AGAIN

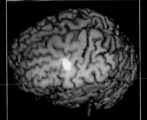 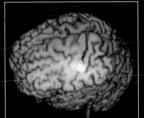

**BEFORE MOVEMENT**
MEG scans show brain activity
as it happens. These two scans
of the left side of the brain show
the activity of groups of neurons
involved in moving the right
index finger. In the first scan,
just milliseconds before the
person moves the finger, neurons
in the left motor cortex become
active (pink) as they send
instructions to finger muscles.

**DURING MOVEMENT**
In the second scan, just
40 milliseconds after the
instruction to move is sent, an
area of neurons in the sensory
cortex "lights up". This occurs
when these neurons receive
signals from stretch receptors
in finger-moving muscles
to say that the muscles are
contracting, and that the
index finger is moving.

**EACH MOVEMENT
IS REPORTED
TO THE BRAIN**

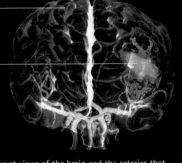

brain

# BRAIN POWER

The brain allows us to think, learn, and be creative – activities that would be impossible if we did not possess a memory. While we forget the vast majority of things we experience, important, impressive events, facts, and skills are stored for up to a lifetime in long-term memory. The limbic system is part of the brain that has a role in memory formation and enables us to experience emotions. Sleep is a state of altered consciousness. It allows the body to rest and the brain to process the information it has taken in during the day, including the formation of memories.

*Cingulate gyrus* modifies behaviour and emotions

*Putamen* stores skills

*Thalamus*

*Prefrontal cortex* holds short-term memories

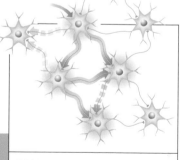

*Olfactory bulb* relays smell input to limbic system

*Amygdala* stores fears and phobias

*Temporal lobe* stores semantic memories

## LIMBIC SYSTEM ►

Deep inside the brain, the limbic system (blue) is a collection of structures, curving around the top of the brain stem. These control emotions such as anger and happiness, protect us from hazards, and play a part in memory. For example, the amygdala assesses dangers and produces fear, and the hippocampus enables us to store and retrieve memories.

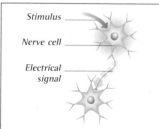

## ◄ MAKING MEMORIES

The making of memories involves several stages. Sensory memory retains fleeting impressions such as sights, sounds, and smells for only a few seconds. Some sensory memories pass into short-term (or working) memory, which handles whatever is being thought about at the time – most of which is then forgotten. But when an event, such as a visit to a fairground, makes a vivid impression, it creates a strong pattern of neuronal activity that, over time, becomes a long-term memory.

e▸▸
memory and sleep

## HOW A MEMORY IS FORMED

**CONNECTION**
Every experience we have is produced by brain neurons firing in a specific pattern. For a long-term memory to form, a pattern of neuron firing that has entered short-term memory must be repeated. When a neuron receives a strong stimulus, it sends a nerve impulse to a neighbouring neuron.

*Stimulus*
*Nerve cell*
*Electrical signal*

**LINKS FORM**
The nerve impulses sent to neighbouring neurons make those cells more responsive to the neuron that sent them. A temporary bond forms between the cells so they are more likely to fire together in future. Further nerve impulses sent to other neighbours draws in more neurons. A pattern of neurons is being created.

*Electrical signal*
*Temporary bond*

**STRONGER LINKS**
With repeated firing, which occurs whenever an event is recalled, the neurons in the group become more firmly connected. Now the neurons will always fire together, whichever is triggered first. These bonds are more likely to develop when something makes a bold impression, such as a tall clown at a fair.

*Permanent bond*

**EXPANDING WEB**
With further repetition, other clusters of neurons are pulled into the network to form a web that represents the full long-term memory. The more complex the web, the more accessible and enduring the memory will be. Each cell cluster represents a different aspect and another route to retrieving the whole memory.

## THE TALL CLOWN ►

Of all the spectacles at the fair, the tall clown with the big hat made the biggest impression on an already excited child. At every opportunity she returned to look at the clown, causing rapid activity in a group of neurons. After telling friends and family about the clown repeatedly, and drawing a picture of him, details pass into her long-term memory. Whenever that particular cluster of cells fires, the experience of the clown is replayed.

*Hippocampus is vital for memory*

*Cerebellum controls movement and balance*

## LONG-TERM MEMORY

### PROCEDURAL
Procedural memories are skills, such as riding a bike or playing a piano, that are learned through practice. They are stored in the putamen – part of the brain that deals with complex movement. Without procedural memory, toddlers would forget how to walk and teenagers how to use a mobile phone.

### SEMANTIC
Stored in the temporal lobe of each cerebral hemisphere, semantic memory deals with learned words, language, facts and their meanings, and the way we use them to understand the world around us. To read or write, we must hold the meaning of words or symbols in semantic memory.

### EPISODIC
Located in areas throughout the cortex, episodic memory records specific events, such as the first day at a new school, a family wedding, or an exciting holiday. Looking at photographs is one way to "jog" our episodic memory to recall the main events of a particular time.

### WORKING MEMORY ▶
Working, or short-term, memory enables us to hold on briefly to the sights, sounds, and other sensations that we experience long enough to act on them. If told a phone number, for example, we hold it in short-term memory long enough to dial the number. Short-term memory also acts as a "scratch pad" that holds partial solutions to problems and keeps track of the ideas in a sentence as we read. Most short-term memories are kept for only seconds and then lost, but more important ones are shunted via the hippocampus into long-term memory.

### FEAR AND PHOBIAS

Fear is a natural part of everyday life and useful because it protects us from harmful situations. But in some people, fear of particular objects or situations is out of all proportion to any possible threat. Common irrational fears, called phobias, include the fear of mice (below), spiders, flying, or being in open spaces. In severe cases, a phobia disrupts normal life, but sufferers can seek help to lessen its effect.

### ◀ SLEEP PATTERNS
Most adults sleep for seven to eight hours a night while school-age children need up to ten hours. Sleep consists of repeated cycles of non-REM (non-rapid eye movement) sleep and REM (rapid eye movement) sleep. The proportion of REM sleep increases through the night. Non-REM sleep consists of four stages of increasing depth. EEG traces record and reveal how brain waves – the patterns of electrical activity of brain cells – alter during sleep cycles.

| STAGE OF SLEEP |
| AWAKE |
| REM |
| NREM (STAGE 1) |
| NREM (STAGE 2) |
| NREM (STAGE 3) |
| NREM (STAGE 4) |

HOURS OF SLEEP
0  1  2  3  4  5  6  7  8  9

### ▲ NREM SLEEP: STAGE 1
During light sleep, the EEG pattern shows peaks (alpha waves), also seen when a person is awake but relaxed.

### ▲ NREM SLEEP: STAGE 2
As sleep deepens, the sleeper is more difficult to wake, and the EEG pattern gets more irregular. The sleeper still moves around.

### ▲ NREM SLEEP: STAGE 3
Although the sleeper moves, his breathing rate, heart rate, and body temperature decrease. Deep sleep delta waves appear.

### ▲ NREM SLEEP: STAGE 4
In very deep sleep, delta waves dominate the EEG. Brain activity is low, and breathing and heart rates fall to a minimum.

### ▲ REM SLEEP
Alpha waves appear, indicating brain activity. The sleeper cannot move, but his eyes dart around while he is dreaming.

# CHEMICAL MESSAGES

The endocrine system, like the nervous system, controls many of the body's functions. It is made up of a scattering of glands in the upper body that release hormones – chemical messages that travel in the bloodstream and regulate activities such as growth and reproduction. The pituitary is the endocrine's master gland, releasing hormones that trigger other glands to secrete hormones of their own.

**ENDOCRINE GLANDS ►**

The endocrine glands are located in the head, neck, and trunk. Some, such as the thyroid gland, are endocrine organs in their own right. Others, such as the pancreas, ovaries, and testes, have other functions, too. The arrows (see key in box below) show the actions of pituitary hormones.

## PITUITARY GLAND HORMONES

### GROWTH HORMONE

Somatotropin, or growth hormone, enables the body both to grow and repair itself. It stimulates most body cells to divide and increase in size, although its main targets are skeletal muscles and bones. During childhood, growth hormone stimulates the replacement of cartilage by bone.

### FSH AND LH

Follicle-stimulating hormone (FSH) and luteinizing hormone (LH) stimulate the reproductive system. In women, they trigger the development and release of eggs from the ovaries and the secretion of the sex hormone, oestrogen. In men, they stimulate sperm production and the release of testosterone.

### ADH

Anti-diuretic hormone (ADH) stimulates nephrons in the kidneys to reabsorb more water into the blood. This reduces the volume of urine released, so helping to maintain the body's normal water balance. ADH is released when the hypothalamus detects a fall in the blood's water content.

### ACTH

Adrenocorticotrophic hormone (ACTH) acts on the outer part (cortex) of the adrenal glands, stimulating them to secrete steroid hormones that help regulate metabolism, assist in controlling levels of water and salts in blood, and, most importantly, help the body react to stress.

### TSH

Thyroid-stimulating hormone (TSH) stimulates the thyroid gland to release two hormones that together regulate metabolic rate and growth. These are thyroxine (described opposite) and tri-iodothyronine. Like other anterior lobe hormones, TSH release is stimulated by the hypothalamus.

### OXYTOCIN

Secreted by the hypothalamus and released by the posterior lobe of the pituitary gland, oxytocin acts in two ways on a woman's body. During labour, it makes the wall of the uterus contract. After birth, it stimulates the breasts to release milk when a baby suckles.

### PROLACTIN

In women, this anterior lobe hormone stimulates the production of milk by the mammary glands in the breasts just before, and after, the birth of a baby. Its release is stimulated by prolactin-releasing hormone (PRH) from the hypothalamus. PRH release is stimulated by breast-feeding.

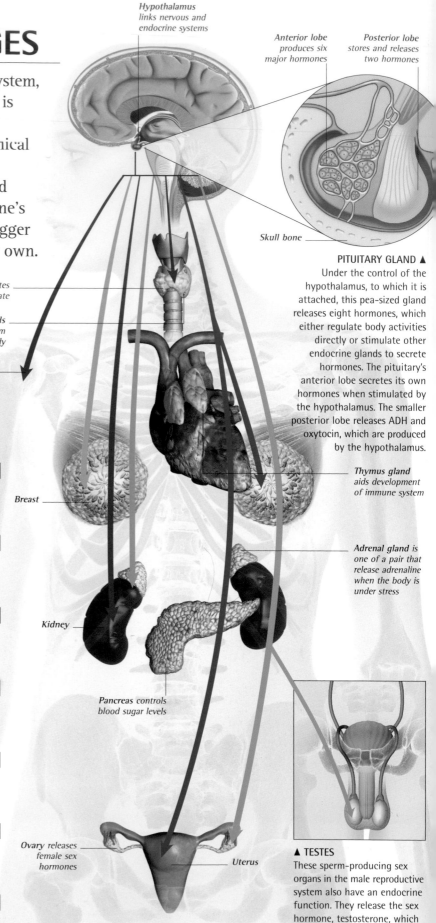

*Hypothalamus links nervous and endocrine systems*

*Anterior lobe produces six major hormones*

*Posterior lobe stores and releases two hormones*

*Skull bone*

**PITUITARY GLAND ▲**

Under the control of the hypothalamus, to which it is attached, this pea-sized gland releases eight hormones, which either regulate body activities directly or stimulate other endocrine glands to secrete hormones. The pituitary's anterior lobe secretes its own hormones when stimulated by the hypothalamus. The smaller posterior lobe releases ADH and oxytocin, which are produced by the hypothalamus.

*Thyroid gland regulates metabolic rate*

*Parathyroid glands help control calcium levels in the body*

*Growth hormone stimulates body cells to grow and divide*

*Breast*

*Thymus gland aids development of immune system*

*Adrenal gland is one of a pair that release adrenaline when the body is under stress*

*Kidney*

*Pancreas controls blood sugar levels*

*Ovary releases female sex hormones*

*Uterus*

**▲ TESTES**

These sperm-producing sex organs in the male reproductive system also have an endocrine function. They release the sex hormone, testosterone, which is essential to sperm production and male characteristics such as facial hair and body shape.

## NEGATIVE FEEDBACK

Hormones work by altering the activity of specific target cells. Changes inside the cells are triggered by the hormone binding to a receptor either inside or on the surface of the target cell.

The level of each hormone in the blood needs to be carefully controlled so that it does not exert too great or too little an effect on target cells. This is achieved by negative feedback systems, which automatically regulate hormone release. One is illustrated here, using the thyroid hormone thyroxine as an example. Thyroxine targets most body cells and increases their metabolic rate. Its release is controlled by another hormone, thyroid-stimulating hormone (TSH), which is released by the pituitary gland.

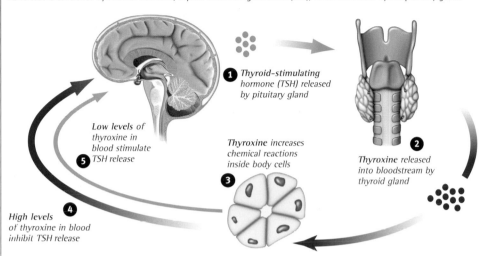

**1** *Thyroid-stimulating hormone (TSH) released by pituitary gland*

*Low levels of thyroxine in blood stimulate TSH release*
**5**

*Thyroxine increases chemical reactions inside body cells*
**3**

*Thyroxine released into bloodstream by thyroid gland*
**2**

*High levels of thyroxine in blood inhibit TSH release*
**4**

**1** PITUITARY GLAND

The hypothalamus secretes thyrotropin-releasing factor (TRH), which stimulates the pituitary gland to release thyroid-stimulating hormone (TSH).

**2** THYROID GLAND

TSH activates the thyroid gland and stimulates it to secrete thyroxine, which is carried by the blood to all parts of the body.

**3** BODY CELLS

Thyroxine binds to the surface of target cells and increases the rate of chemical reactions inside them. This increases the body's metabolic rate.

**4** HIGH LEVELS

When blood levels of thyroxine are high, the hypothalamus slows release of TRH. Secretion of TSH by the pituitary gland decreases, and the thyroid reduces its production of thyroxine.

**5** LOW LEVELS

If thyroxine levels in the bloodstream are low, TRH release increases, as does TSH production, so more thyroxine is secreted by the thyroid.

---

### PANCREATIC HORMONES ▶

The pancreas has two roles. Acinar cells release digestive enzymes, while clusters of cells called islets of Langerhans release the hormones insulin and glucagon. Insulin lowers and glucagon raises glucose levels in the blood. Between them these hormones ensure a stable level of blood glucose so that cells have a constant supply of fuel.

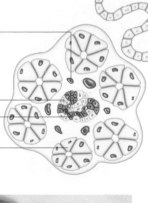

*Islet of Langerhans secretes hormones into bloodstream*

*Blood vessels carry hormones out of pancreas*

*Beta cells secrete insulin*
*Alpha cells secrete glucagon*

*Acinar cells secrete digestive enzymes into ducts*

*Pupils get wider to let more light into the eyes*

*Heart rate increases to pump more blood to muscles*

*Blood flow to muscles increases*

*Breathing rate increases to get more oxygen into the blood*

*Glucose level in blood increases*

hormones

### ▲ FIGHT OR FLIGHT

When a person is threatened or under stress, as the man above undoubtedly is, the body reacts quickly. Nerve impulses stimulate the adrenal glands to release adrenaline. Unlike other hormones, adrenaline acts fast to boost heart and breathing rates, increase levels of energy-rich glucose in the blood, and divert extra blood to the muscles. These changes ensure that the muscles get the extra energy needed for the body to either confront the threat or run away. This is known as the fight or flight reaction.

### USING INSULIN ▶

In some people the pancreas secretes little or no insulin, causing a disorder called diabetes. Without insulin, levels of glucose in the blood cannot be controlled, and cells do not get the fuel they need. People with diabetes can inject insulin to keep their blood glucose under control. Some use an insulin pen (right), which supplies a measured dose.

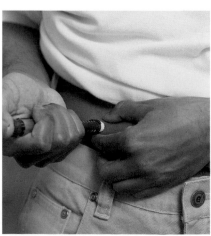

# CIRCULATION

Pumped by the heart, blood circulates around the body, delivering oxygen, food, and hormones to all body cells and removing wastes. Together the heart, blood vessels, and blood make up the circulatory system. Arteries carry oxygen-rich blood from the heart to tissues, while veins carry oxygen-poor blood back to the heart. (The only reversal of these roles is in the circulation between the heart and lungs.) The body's main circulation takes a figure-of-eight path, picking up oxygen from the lungs and delivering it to body tissues via a network of tiny capillaries.

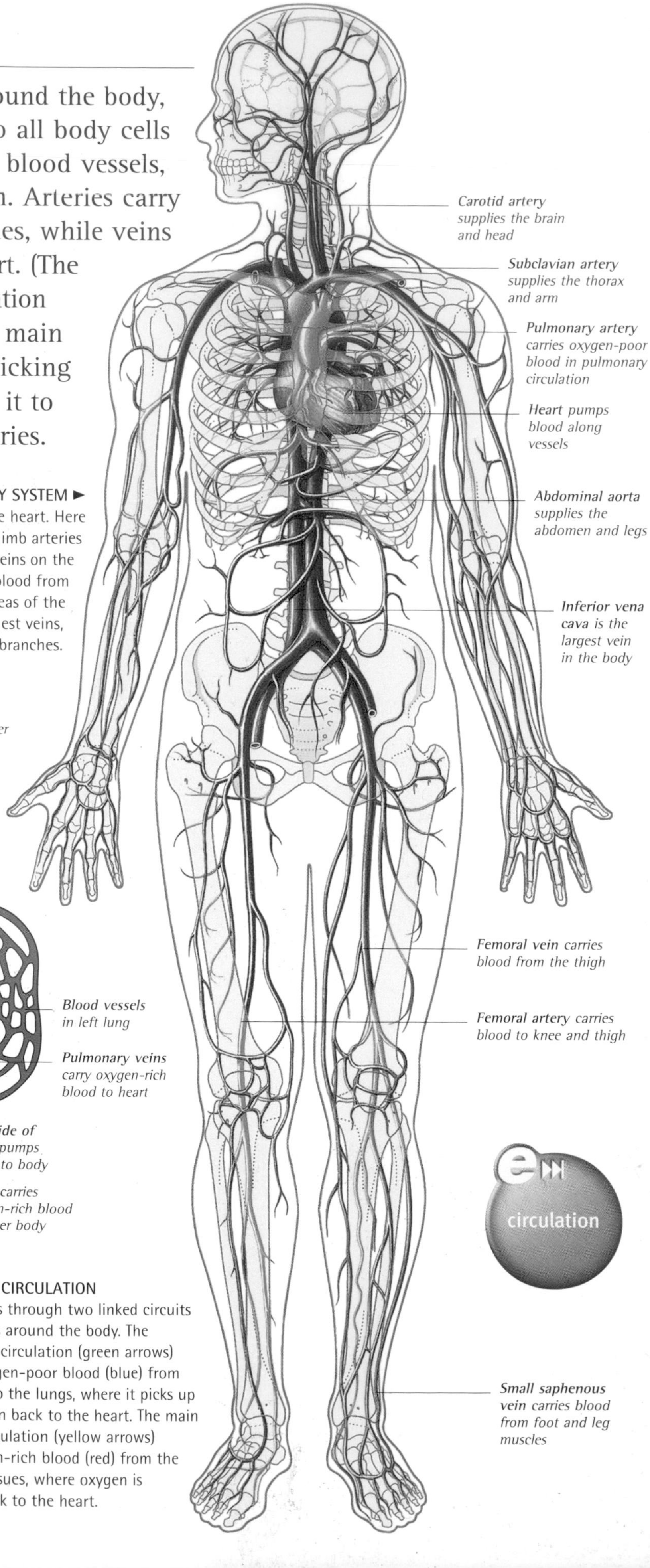

**CIRCULATORY SYSTEM ▶**

Blood vessels extend to all parts of the body from the heart. Here the body's major blood vessels are shown with major limb arteries on the right-hand side of the body, and major limb veins on the left. The aorta – the body's largest artery – carries blood from the heart and branches to supply blood to all areas of the body. The superior and inferior vena cava, the largest veins, bring blood back to the heart from numerous vein branches.

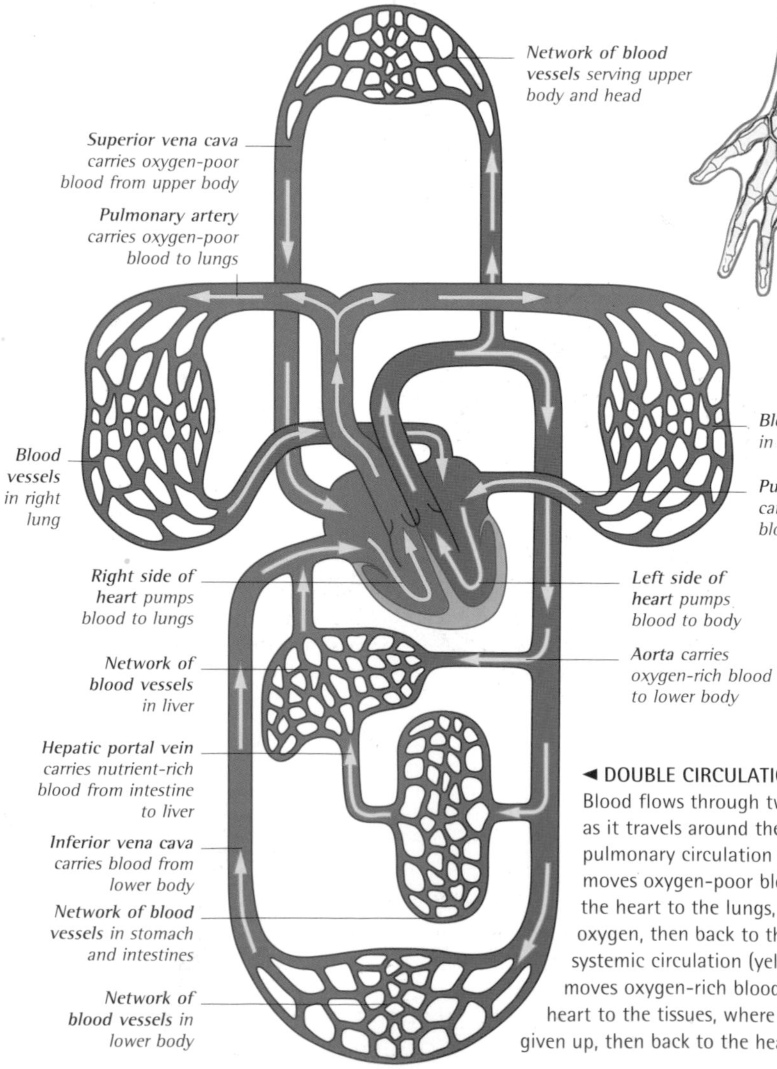

*Carotid artery supplies the brain and head*

*Subclavian artery supplies the thorax and arm*

*Pulmonary artery carries oxygen-poor blood in pulmonary circulation*

*Heart pumps blood along vessels*

*Abdominal aorta supplies the abdomen and legs*

*Inferior vena cava is the largest vein in the body*

*Network of blood vessels serving upper body and head*

*Superior vena cava carries oxygen-poor blood from upper body*

*Pulmonary artery carries oxygen-poor blood to lungs*

*Blood vessels in right lung*

*Blood vessels in left lung*

*Pulmonary veins carry oxygen-rich blood to heart*

*Right side of heart pumps blood to lungs*

*Left side of heart pumps blood to body*

*Network of blood vessels in liver*

*Aorta carries oxygen-rich blood to lower body*

*Hepatic portal vein carries nutrient-rich blood from intestine to liver*

*Inferior vena cava carries blood from lower body*

*Network of blood vessels in stomach and intestines*

*Network of blood vessels in lower body*

*Femoral vein carries blood from the thigh*

*Femoral artery carries blood to knee and thigh*

**◀ DOUBLE CIRCULATION**

Blood flows through two linked circuits as it travels around the body. The pulmonary circulation (green arrows) moves oxygen-poor blood (blue) from the heart to the lungs, where it picks up oxygen, then back to the heart. The main systemic circulation (yellow arrows) moves oxygen-rich blood (red) from the heart to the tissues, where oxygen is given up, then back to the heart.

*Small saphenous vein carries blood from foot and leg muscles*

e▶▶
circulation

# TYPES OF BLOOD VESSEL

*Inner lining*  *Elastic layer*

*Thick muscle layer*

**ARTERY**
Arteries carry blood from the heart to the tissues. The tough, elastic, and relatively thick wall of an artery enables it to resist the pulses of high-pressure blood that passes along it with every heartbeat. It expands as the heart contracts and forces blood into it, then recoils to push blood onwards as the heart relaxes. We feel the pressure wave produced by these actions as a pulse.

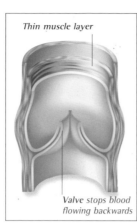

*Thin muscle layer*

*Valve stops blood flowing backwards*

**VEIN**
Veins carry blood from the tissues to the heart. The wall of a vein is thinner with a narrower muscle layer than that of an artery of the same size because it does not have to withstand high blood pressure. Low pressure inside veins means that blood tends to flow away from the heart. But valves inside veins prevent this by opening to let blood flow towards the heart and closing if it flows backwards.

*Very thin wall made of a single cell layer*

**CAPILLARY**
The most numerous of all blood vessels, capillaries carry blood between arteries and veins. The wall of the capillary consists of a layer of smooth endothelium, just one cell thick. The capillary wall is "leaky", allowing liquid to pass in and out of the blood. White blood cells are able to squeeze between endothelial cells to migrate into the tissues and fight infection.

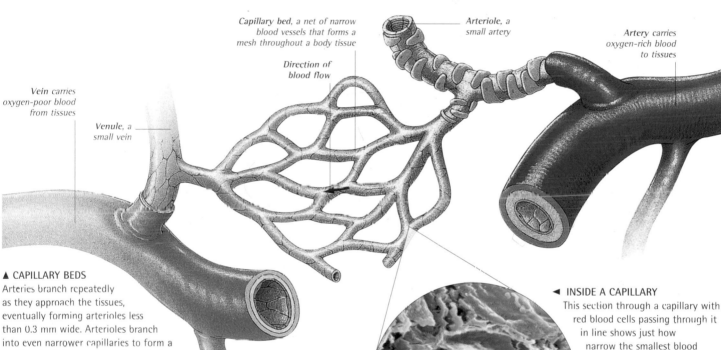

*Capillary bed*, a net of narrow blood vessels that forms a mesh throughout a body tissue

*Direction of blood flow*

*Arteriole*, a small artery

*Artery* carries oxygen-rich blood to tissues

*Vein* carries oxygen-poor blood from tissues

*Venule*, a small vein

## ▲ CAPILLARY BEDS
Arteries branch repeatedly as they approach the tissues, eventually forming arterioles less than 0.3 mm wide. Arterioles branch into even narrower capillaries to form a capillary bed that can pass through tissue. Capillaries emerge from the tissues and join with tiny veins called venules. These connect with larger veins to carry oxygen-poor blood back to the heart.

## ◄ INSIDE A CAPILLARY
This section through a capillary with red blood cells passing through it in line shows just how narrow the smallest blood vessels actually are. It also shows the thinness and "leakiness" of capillary walls. These allow oxygen, nutrients, and other substances to pass out of the capillary and through tissue fluid to tissue cells. Waste and other substances are also able to leak through in the opposite direction.

## ◄ IMAGING BLOOD VESSELS
Magnetic resonance angiography (MRA), a type of MRI, is a recent development. It provides clear images of blood vessels so that problems, such as blockages and tears in arteries and veins, can be detected more easily. Before the scan is carried out, a substance can be injected into the bloodstream to make the vessels clearer. This MRA scan shows a 3-D view of the major chest blood vessels including the aortic arch (top, centre).

## BLOOD VESSEL FACTS

| | |
|---|---|
| Total length of body's blood vessels | 50,000 km (31,000 miles) |
| Number of times blood vessels would wrap around Earth | 4 |
| Percentage of total length made up by capillaries | 98% |
| External diameter of largest artery (aorta) | 25 mm (1 in) |
| Exernal diameter of largest vein (vena cava) | 25 mm (1 in) |
| Average diameter of a capillary | 0.008 mm |
| Average length of a capillary | 1 mm |

# BEATING HEART

The fist-sized heart lies in the thorax between, and partially overlapped by, the two lungs. It is at the centre of the circulatory system, working tirelessly for a lifetime to pump blood around the body. The heart consists of two muscular pumps joined side by side. The right side receives oxygen-poor blood from the tissues and pumps it to the lungs to pick up oxygen. The left side receives oxygen-rich blood from the lungs and pumps it to the tissues to deliver oxygen. Contraction of the two sides occurs together in a three-stage heartbeat cycle, controlled by a pacemaker.

*Aorta carries oxygen-rich blood to the body*

*Superior vena cava carries oxygen-poor blood from the upper body to the right atrium*

## INSIDE THE HEART ▶

The internal structure of the heart, seen here, shows the two sides separated completely by a muscular septum. Each side has two chambers – an upper, smaller, thin-walled atrium, and a lower, larger, thick-walled ventricle. Blood flows into the heart through the atria, from atria into ventricles, and is then pumped out of the heart by the ventricles. Contraction is produced by cardiac muscle fibres in the heart's wall.

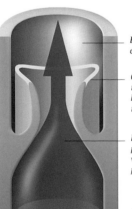

heart

*Right atrium receives oxygen-poor blood from the inferior and superior venae cavae*

## HEART VALVE ▶

Four valves maintain a one-way flow of blood through each side of the heart by preventing backflow. Bicuspid and tricuspid valves lie between atria and ventricles, and semilunar valves (right) guard the exits from the ventricles. When valves close, they produce "lub-dup" heart sounds that can be heard using a stethoscope. Bicuspid and tricuspid valves produce the long, loud "lub" sound, while semilunar valves make the short, sharp "dup" sound.

*Right ventricle pumps blood to the lungs*

*Inferior vena cava*

*Blood flows easily forwards*

*Cusps of valve forced open by blood pressure from behind*

*High blood pressure behind valve as heart pumps*

*Blood cannot flow back; it is trapped in front of valve by closed cusps*

*Cusps of valve forced shut by blood pressure in front of valve*

*Low blood pressure as heart rests between beats*

## ▲ CONTROLLING BLOOD FLOW

These diagrams show the workings of the semilunar valves, which guard the exits from the right and left ventricles. Each valve contains pocket-like cusps. When the ventricles contract, the cusps flatten, and high pressure blood flows between them. When the ventricles relax, blood trying to flow back into the heart fills the cusps, forcing the valves shut.

## HEART STRINGS ▶

These fibrous cords, known as heart strings, attach the valve flaps to the wall of each ventricle. The tricuspid valve on the right of the heart stops blood flowing from the right ventricle into the right atrium. The bicuspid valve does the same job for the left ventricle. When the ventricle contracts, blood pressure pushes the valve flaps closed. The heart strings tighten to prevent the valves turning inside out like an umbrella in a gale.

*Pulmonary artery carries oxygen-poor blood from the right ventricle to the lungs*

*Left atrium receives oxygen-rich blood from the pulmonary veins*

*Pulmonary veins carry oxygen-rich blood from the lungs to the heart*

*Aortic semilunar valve stops blood flowing backwards into the heart from the aorta*

*Bicuspid valve stops backflow of blood into the left atrium when the left ventricle contracts*

*Left ventricle has thicker wall than right because it has to pump blood further*

*Septum is the wall that divides the heart into left and right halves*

*Myocardium is thick cardiac muscle layer in heart wall*

*Pericardium is tough membrane around heart*

*Apex is tip of heart*

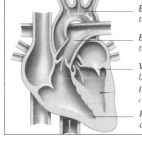

## HEARTBEAT SEQUENCE

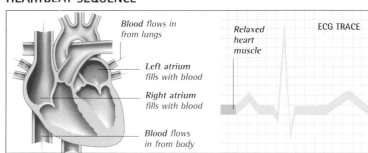

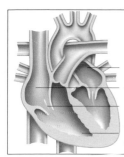

*Blood flows in from lungs*

*Left atrium fills with blood*

*Right atrium fills with blood*

*Blood flows in from body*

*Relaxed heart muscle* — ECG TRACE

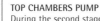

### RELAXED HEART
This sequence shows what happens in the heart during each stage of contraction. The electrical activity of the heart – shown as an ECG trace – follows the signal from a pacemaker through the atria and then the ventricles. During the first stage of contraction, called diastole, both atria and ventricles relax, and blood enters the atria.

*Left atrium squeezes*

*Right atrium squeezes*

*Valves open; blood flows into ventricles*

*Ventricles fill with blood*

*Atria contract* — ECG TRACE

### TOP CHAMBERS PUMP
During the second stage of the cycle, called atrial systole, the atria contract together and pump blood into the ventricles, forcing open the bicuspid and tricuspid valves. The semilunar valves remain closed to prevent backflow. The small peak on the ECG shows contraction, which is triggered by signals passing through the walls of the atria.

*Blood pumped to body*

*Blood pumped to lungs*

*Valves closed by blood pressure*

*Left ventricle contracts*

*Right ventricle contracts*

*Delayed impulse* — ECG TRACE — *Ventricles contract*

### BOTTOM CHAMBERS PUMP
After a tiny pause, the final stage, called ventricular systole, begins. As both ventricles contract to pump blood out of the heart, the semilunar valves open, and the bicuspid and tricuspid valves close to prevent backflow. The large peak on the ECG shows the flow of electrical signals through the ventricle walls just before contraction.

*Right coronary artery*

*Branch of left coronary artery*

### ◄ THE HEART'S OWN BLOOD SUPPLY
The heart's cardiac muscle needs a constant supply of oxygen and food to supply the energy it needs to contract. The blood that gushes through its chambers cannot meet these demands, so the heart has its own blood supply – provided by the blood vessels shown left. Left and right coronary arteries arise from the aorta and branch to form capillaries that pass through muscle. These emerge to form veins that eventually empty into the right atrium.

*Angioplasty balloon forces open a narrowed artery*

*Stent is a mesh of fine wire that holds the artery open afterwards*

### TREATMENT FOR HEART DISEASE ▲
The build-up of fatty deposits in blood vessels reduces the blood flow to the heart, which can lead to a heart attack. Coronary artery disease is treated by balloon angioplasty, in which a deflated balloon catheter is introduced into the narrowed blood vessel and inflated to widen it. A metal stent may be left in place to keep the artery open.

*Dual-chamber pacemaker implanted in shoulder*

*Wire stimulating the heart's atrium*

*Wire stimulating the heart's ventricle*

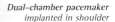

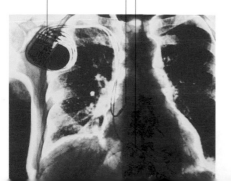

### SETTING THE PACE ►
The heart has its own pacemaker in the right atrium which sends out regular electrical signals to its muscle fibres. This sets the rate at which the heart beats, and responds to changes in the body's activity. If this stops working normally, an artificial battery-powered pacemaker (right) can be implanted. Here, wires carry electrical signals to both an atrium and a ventricle to set the rate of contraction.

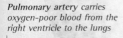

# INSIDE BLOOD

Pumped by the heart, blood is a red, liquid tissue that flows around the body to supply its trillions of cells with all their needs. Its main roles are transport, defence, and the distribution of heat. Blood delivers oxygen, food, and other essentials to cells and removes their wastes. It defends the body by destroying pathogens – invading micro-organisms that cause disease. By distributing heat it helps keep the body at a constant 37°C (98.6°F). Blood also clots to prevent life-threatening leakage while damaged blood vessels heal.

| BLOOD FACTS | |
|---|---|
| Average volume of blood in an adult | 5 litres (9 pt) |
| Number of red blood cells in a 50 mm³ drop of blood | 250,000,000 |
| Number of white blood cells in a 50 mm³ drop of blood | 375,000 |
| Number of platelets in a 50 mm³ drop of blood | 16,000,000 |
| Production rate of red blood cells by bone marrow | 2 million/second |
| Life span of red blood cell | 120 days |
| Haemoglobin molecules inside one red blood cell | 250 million |
| Oxygen molecules carried by one haemoglobin molecule | 4 |
| Oxygen molecules carried by fully loaded red blood cell | 1 billion |

*Red blood cell* has a dimpled shape and no nucleus

*Neutrophil* tracks down and eats pathogens

*Lymphocyte* releases chemicals called antibodies that mark specific pathogens for destruction

*Platelets* are cell fragments rather than cells

**▲ INGREDIENTS OF BLOOD**
Blood consists of a liquid called plasma in which various types of blood cells are suspended. Plasma is 90 per cent water, the other 10 per cent being made up of nutrients such as glucose, hormones, salts, proteins such as fibrinogen, and wastes such as carbon dioxide. Red blood cells transport oxygen from the lungs to the tissues. White blood cells, such as neutrophils and lymphocytes, destroy bacteria and other germs.

## BLOOD COMPOSITION ▶
If blood is poured into a glass tube and spun in a centrifuge, its main components separate into three layers. The sizes of these layers indicate the amount of each component by volume. Yellow-coloured plasma makes up 55 per cent of blood, white blood cells and platelets less than 1 per cent, and red blood cells just over 44 per cent.

*Plasma*

*White blood cells and platelets*

*Red blood cells*

*Neutrophil nucleus has many lobes linked by narrow connections*

blood

HAEMOGLOBIN

*Oxygen picked up in lungs*

*Oxygen sticks to iron atom in haem and makes oxyhaemoglobin*

*Haem part of haemoglobin includes an iron atom and attracts oxygen*

OXYHAEMOGLOBIN

*Oxygen splits from oxyhaemoglobin and passes into tissues*

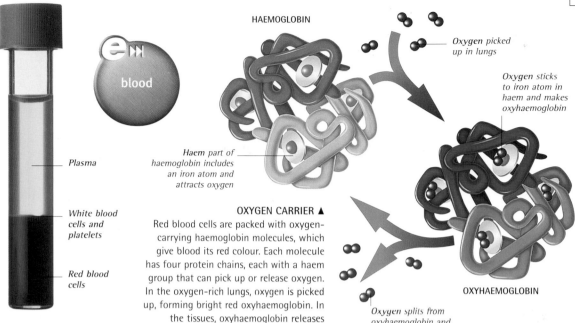

## OXYGEN CARRIER ▲
Red blood cells are packed with oxygen-carrying haemoglobin molecules, which give blood its red colour. Each molecule has four protein chains, each with a haem group that can pick up or release oxygen. In the oxygen-rich lungs, oxygen is picked up, forming bright red oxyhaemoglobin. In the tissues, oxyhaemoglobin releases oxygen to form dark red haemoglobin.

## TESTING BLOOD
Blood tests are used routinely by doctors to diagnose disease or monitor general health. A blood sample is analysed to check whether levels of one or more of the chemicals in plasma are normal. The test below measures levels of glucose, the body's main energy supply. A drop of blood is dabbed onto a glucose-sensitive pad on the test strip, which changes colour according to how much glucose is present. High levels may indicate that a person has diabetes, the inability of the body to use glucose normally.

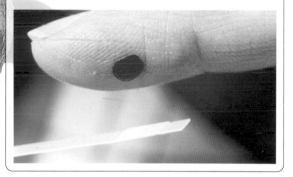

## WOUND HEALING

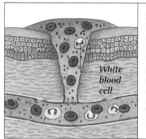

**INJURY**
This section through skin and one of its blood vessels shows blood escaping through a cut to the skin's surface. White blood cells seek out any invading micro-organisms, and the blood's repair system, called clotting, moves into action to prevent blood loss. The same system seals damaged blood vessels deeper in the body.

*White blood cell*

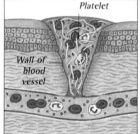

**PLUG**
In the first part of the repair, the damage to the blood vessel and its surrounding tissues causes platelets, which normally flow easily through the blood vessel, to become spiky and stick to each other and the damaged blood vessel wall. The spiky platelets attract more platelets, forming a plug that stops blood loss temporarily.

*Platelet*

*Wall of blood vessel*

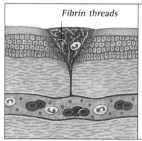

**CLOT**
Platelets and damaged tissues release chemicals that turn blood into a jelly-like clot. Within minutes, these chemicals convert the blood protein fibrinogen into insoluble fibrin. Net-like fibrin traps red blood cells to form a clot that reinforces the platelet plug. As the clot becomes tighter, it pulls the torn edges of the blood vessel together.

*Fibrin threads*

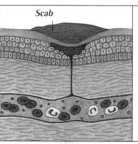

**SCAB**
In the final stage of healing, the wall of the damaged blood vessel repairs itself, as does the surrounding tissue. Clot-busting chemicals remove the clot now that its job is done. Where injury occurs at the skin's surface, as here, the outer part of the clot forms a protective scab. This dries and falls off once healing is complete.

*Scab*

## BLOOD GROUPS ▶
Every person has one of four blood groups – A, B, AB, or O – the names relate to markers (antigens) on red blood cells. Group AB, for example, has A and B antigens, while group O has none. In three of the groups, blood plasma also carries up to two antibodies to other blood types. If "foreign" blood enters the body, the antibodies bind to foreign antigens causing blood cells to clump together and block blood vessels. That is why blood types must be matched during transfusions.

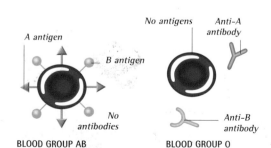

*Anti-B antibody* — *A antigen*
**BLOOD GROUP A**

*B antigen* — *Anti-A antibody*
**BLOOD GROUP B**

*A antigen* — *B antigen* — *No antibodies*
**BLOOD GROUP AB**

*No antigens* — *Anti-A antibody* — *Anti-B antibody*
**BLOOD GROUP O**

# DISEASE AND DEFENCE

Diseases occur when one or more parts of the body stops working properly. Infectious diseases, such as colds and measles, are caused by micro-organisms called pathogens, which invade the body. These include types of bacteria, viruses, and protists. The body has a number of defences to prevent pathogens invading and growing inside (infecting) it. Outer defences include physical barriers such as the skin, and chemicals contained in tears and saliva. Pathogens that manage to penetrate these defences are usually tracked down and destroyed by pathogen-eating white blood cells. Non-infectious diseases, such as lung cancer, have a variety of different causes.

## BODY INVADERS

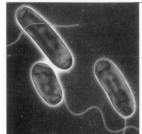

### BACTERIA
Simple, single-celled organisms, bacteria are the most abundant of all living things. The majority of bacteria are harmless to humans. However, *Legionella* (left), which causes a type of pneumonia called Legionnaires' disease, is one of a number of disease-causing bacteria. Food poisoning and meningitis are also caused by bacteria.

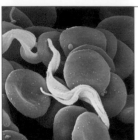

### PROTISTS
A trypanosome (yellow) wriggles among red blood cells in a blood sample. Trypanosomes belong to a group of single-celled organisms called protists. Most protists live freely in oceans and freshwater, but some cause disease. Trypanosomes cause the disease known as sleeping sickness. Another protist, called Plasmodium, is the cause of malaria.

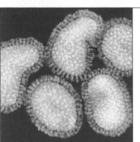

### VIRUSES
The smallest of all microbes, viruses are non-living chemical packages that neither feed nor grow and which have to invade a living cell in order to reproduce. Several viruses cause disease in humans including the flu virus (left), which causes influenza. Other viral diseases include colds, measles, rubella, chickenpox, mumps, and rabies.

disease

### ▼ PREVENTING ENTRY
Some of the body's most important outer defences are shown below. Tears, saliva, sweat, and sebum contain chemicals that kill bacteria. Stomach acid destroys pathogens in food and drink. Mucus in the airways traps breathed-in microbes, which are swallowed and destroyed in the stomach. In the vagina and on the skin, harmless bacteria prevent disease-causing microbes from settling.

### SALIVA ►
Secreted by the salivary glands, saliva flows into the mouth – especially when we are about to eat, or are eating. Saliva lubricates food during chewing, washes the mouth out, and helps kill the bacteria that cause tooth decay and gum disease.

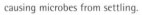

*Salivary duct* surrounded by saliva-secreting cells

### ◄ TEARS
A section through a tear gland shows cells that secrete tears. Tears moisten and wash dirt from the front of the eyeball, and contain lysozyme, a chemical that kills bacteria, protecting the eyeball from infection.

*Secretory cell*

*Teardrop*

### SWEAT AND SEBUM ►
Watery sweat is released from pores like this one onto the surface of the skin. Oily sebum is also secreted onto the skin's surface from glands located in hair follicles. Both sweat and sebum inhibit the growth of harmful bacteria on the skin.

### ◄ MUCUS
This view of the trachea's lining shows the goblet cells that produce mucus. This sticky liquid traps pathogens from breathed-in air, so they do not reach the lungs. Hair-like cilia move the contaminated mucus up to the throat to be swallowed.

*Cilia*  *Goblet cell*

### STOMACH ACID ►
In the lining of the stomach, this opening leads to a gastric gland, which secretes hydrochloric acid, mucus, and enzymes. The powerful acid kills most of the microbes that enter the stomach in food or drink that has just been swallowed.

### ◄ HELPFUL BACTERIA
Rod-shaped *Lactobacillus* bacteria are just some of the bacteria that live harmlessly in a woman's vagina. They make the inside of the vagina slightly acidic, preventing harmful bacterial growth.

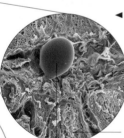

*Lactobacillus* bacteria

◄ CELL EATER

This SEM shows a macrophage (cream) about to destroy some *Borrelia* bacteria (blue) – pathogens that cause Lyme disease in humans. Macrophages (big eaters) are hunter white blood cells, present in many body tissues. They destroy invader cells by eating them in a process called phagocytosis. When the macrophage detects its prey, it sends out extensions (called pseudopodia) that stick to and flow around the pathogens. The macrophage pulls the bacteria inside its own cell, then digests and kills them.

*Macrophage's cell body* sends out projections to surround bacteria

*Bacterium* about to be engulfed by macrophage

## NON-INFECTIOUS DISEASES

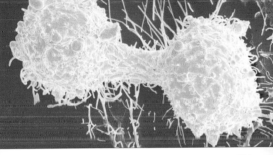

Non-infectious diseases, such as heart disease, diabetes, bronchitis, and cancers, can be the result of a genetic disposition, and/or lifestyle factors, such as smoking, or a fault in a person's immune system. While the body's defences cannot protect against most non-infectious diseases, they can detect and destroy most cancer cells. Cancers are caused when cells, such as these breast cancer cells, multiply out of control, producing tumours that interfere with the workings of the body.

## INFLAMMATION

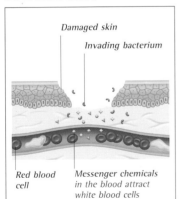

*Damaged skin*

*Invading bacterium*

*Red blood cell*

*Messenger chemicals in the blood attract white blood cells*

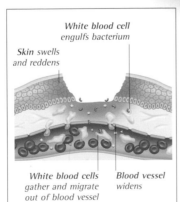

*White blood cell engulfs bacterium*

*Skin swells and reddens*

*White blood cells gather and migrate out of blood vessel*

*Blood vessel widens*

### DAMAGE

Redness, heat, swelling, and pain are the symptoms of inflammation, the body's response to injury or infection. Within minutes of damage occurring, affected cells release histamines and other chemicals. These make blood vessels wider, to increase blood flow to the area, and more leaky, so that defence and repair substances pass more easily into the tissues.

### RESPONSE

As more blood flows into the damaged area, it gets redder and hotter. As more fluid passes out of the blood vessels, the tissue swells. An hour after the damage occurred, phagocytes (microbe-eating white blood cells) surge with full force into the area, engulfing pathogens, and halting their invasion. At the same time, the process of repair begins.

FEVER ►

The symptoms of fever – a high body temperature, accompanied by sweating and shivering – most commonly occur during infection by bacteria or viruses. Increasing the body's temperature above the normal 37°C (98.6°F) slows down bacteria or virus reproduction while increasing the activities of phagocytes – microbe-eating white blood cells. Fever is triggered when white blood cells release chemicals called pyrogens. These reset the body's "thermostat", located in the hypothalamus in the brain.

*Digital thermometer* shows temperature above normal 37°C (98.6°F)

# LYMPH AND IMMUNITY

Running parallel to the blood's circulation, the lymphatic system has a major role in the immune system – the body's defences against harmful invading micro-organisms (pathogens). A network of lymph vessels collect excess fluid (lymph) from tissues and return it to the blood. Pathogens are filtered from the lymph as it passes through lymph nodes. Lymph nodes contain macrophages, which eat pathogens, and white blood cells (lymphocytes), which identify and attack pathogens – either destroying them directly or launching antibodies against them. Vaccines stimulate the immune system so it responds rapidly if the body is invaded by a pathogen such as a flu virus.

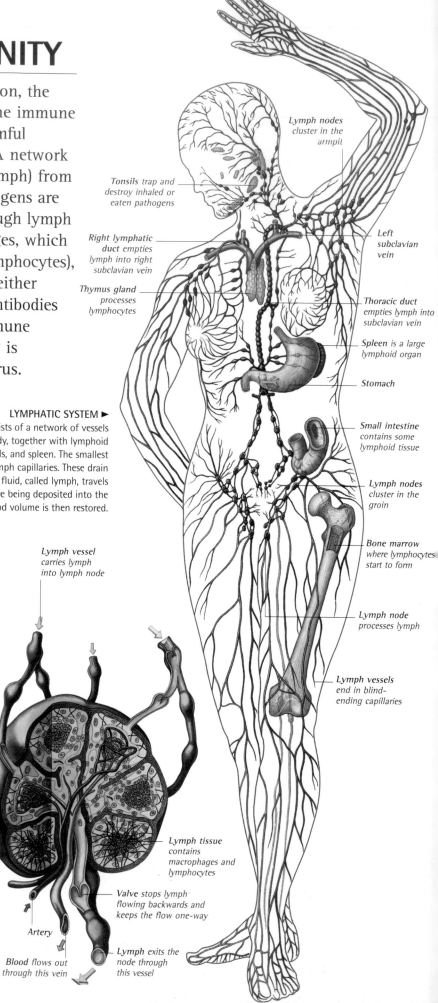

Lymph nodes cluster in the armpit

Tonsils trap and destroy inhaled or eaten pathogens

Right lymphatic duct empties lymph into right subclavian vein

Thymus gland processes lymphocytes

Left subclavian vein

Thoracic duct empties lymph into subclavian vein

Spleen is a large lymphoid organ

Stomach

Small intestine contains some lymphoid tissue

Lymph nodes cluster in the groin

Bone marrow where lymphocytes start to form

Lymph node processes lymph

Lymph vessels end in blind-ending capillaries

**LYMPHATIC SYSTEM ►**

The lymphatic system consists of a network of vessels that extends to all parts of the body, together with lymphoid organs such as the lymph nodes, tonsils, and spleen. The smallest branches of the system are called lymph capillaries. These drain surplus fluid from the tissues. This fluid, called lymph, travels along larger lymphatic vessels before being deposited into the subclavian veins. Normal blood volume is then restored.

Valve stops any backflow of lymph

Tissue fluid flows into leaky lymph capillary

Lymph vessel carries lymph into lymph node

**▲ LYMPH CAPILLARIES**

The smallest, blind-ending branches of the lymphatic system are the lymph capillaries. These pass through tissue cells, much as blood capillaries do. Excess watery fluid located between tissue cells flows into the thin-walled lymph capillaries through tiny flaps that open like one-way swing doors. The fluid, now called lymph, is carried on to larger lymph vessels. Lymph is pushed along the vessels when the skeletal muscles surrounding them contract. Valves prevent any backflow of lymph.

Lymph tissue contains macrophages and lymphocytes

Valve stops lymph flowing backwards and keeps the flow one-way

Artery

Lymph exits the node through this vessel

Blood flows out through this vein

**LYMPH NODE ►**

Small masses of lymph tissue called lymph nodes help to protect the body against infection by acting as a filter for the lymph passing through them. These nodes are found along the length of lymph vessels, as well as areas such as the groin and the armpits. Inside the nodes are macrophages and lymphocytes, which both defend the body. Macrophages destroy infectious micro-organisms, cancer cells, and debris, while lymphocytes launch their immune response against invading pathogens. When lymph nodes are fighting against infection, they sometimes swell – producing "swollen glands".

## IMMUNE RESPONSE

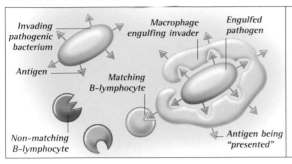

**FIRST PHASE**
Shown here is the response of immune cells called B-lymphocytes when a pathogen invades the body. As the bacteria attack, some are engulfed by macrophages. The macrophage "presents" antigens on the surface of the bacteria to B-lymphocytes. Some B-lymphocytes have a matching receptor on their surface. The antigen fits into this receptor like a key in a lock.

*Invading pathogenic bacterium*
*Antigen*
*Matching B-lymphocyte*
*Macrophage engulfing invader*
*Engulfed pathogen*
*Non-matching B-lymphocyte*
*Antigen being "presented"*

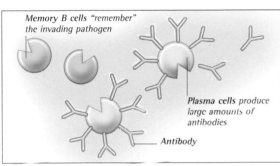

**SECOND PHASE**
Now the B-lymphocytes are activated, they divide to form plasma cells and memory cells. Plasma cells secrete thousands of antibody molecules per second, which are carried by the blood to the site of infection. Memory B cells retain a memory of the antigen. If the bacteria invade again, the cells will divide rapidly to form plasma cells that release antibodies to fight the infection.

*Memory B cells "remember" the invading pathogen*
*Plasma cells produce large amounts of antibodies*
*Antibody*

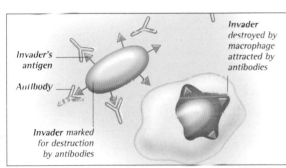

**THIRD PHASE**
Antibodies are Y-shaped molecules with "arms" that are unique to each type of antibody. They bind the antibody to a specific antigen wherever it has invaded the body. Instead of killing the invader, antibodies mark it for destruction by a macrophage. Other lymphocytes, called T-cells, destroy directly, especially cells infected by viruses, or cancer cells.

*Invader's antigen*
*Antibody*
*Invader marked for destruction by antibodies*
*Invader destroyed by macrophage attracted by antibodies*

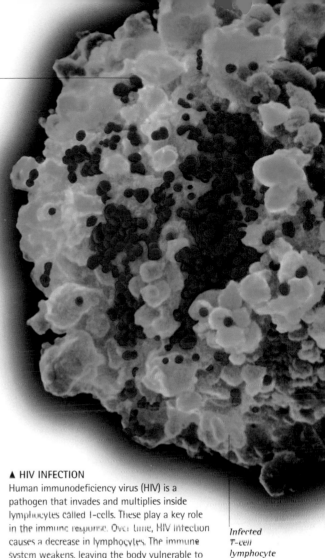

*HIV particles emerging from lymphocyte*

*Infected T-cell lymphocyte*

### ▲ HIV INFECTION
Human immunodeficiency virus (HIV) is a pathogen that invades and multiplies inside lymphocytes called T-cells. These play a key role in the immune response. Over time, HIV infection causes a decrease in lymphocytes. The immune system weakens, leaving the body vulnerable to infections that would not normally cause harm. This multiple assault on the body is known as AIDS (acquired immunodeficiency syndrome) and is usually fatal. However, there are now drugs that can slow HIV infection.

*Vaccine is injected through the skin*

immunity

### ◄ IMMUNIZATION
The immune system destroys most, but not all, infections, and some cause damage while the body fights them. Immunization boosts protection by helping the immune system. In active immunization, a weakened form of a pathogen, such as the measles virus, is injected. This stimulates the release of antibodies against it. Passive immunization involves injecting antibodies to a pathogen to limit the severity of an infection in an unimmunized person.

### HOW ACTIVE IMMUNIZATION WORKS

During active immunization, or vaccination, a harmless form of an infective micro-organism — either weakened or dead — is introduced into the body, usually by the injection of a vaccine. The body's immune system response comes from white blood cells called B-lymphocytes. These react to the pathogen's antigens by secreting antibodies against them and retaining a "memory" of the antigens.

Should the infective micro-organism invade the body later on, the immune system quickly springs into action, releasing antibodies rapidly and in large quantities, so the invader is destroyed before it can infect the body. A different vaccine must be given for each disease because each pathogen stimulates production of a specific antibody. Vaccination has greatly reduced the occurrence of infectious diseases in the Western world, particularly among children.

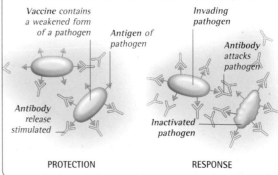

*Vaccine contains a weakened form of a pathogen*
*Antigen of pathogen*
*Antibody release stimulated*
*Invading pathogen*
*Antibody attacks pathogen*
*Inactivated pathogen*

PROTECTION          RESPONSE

# TREATING DISEASE

Disease disrupts the normal working of the human body. Advances in medical science have enabled doctors and other health workers to treat many of the diseases that affect us. Diagnosis determines what is wrong with the patient. This can involve modern hi-tech methods such as CT, MRI, or MRA scans. When treatment is needed, it may be with drugs, surgery, or radiotherapy. Not all diseases are preventable but we can minimize the risk of illness by adopting a healthy lifestyle and by having regular health checks and screening.

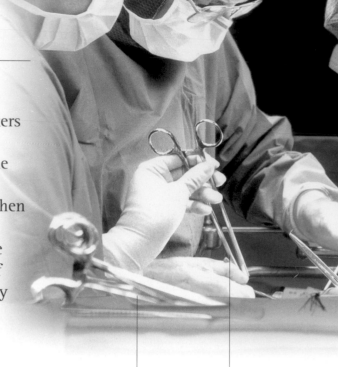

Artery clamp grips blood vessel to prevent bleeding

Instruments are sterilized before surgery begins

Forceps are used for gripping and lifting tissues

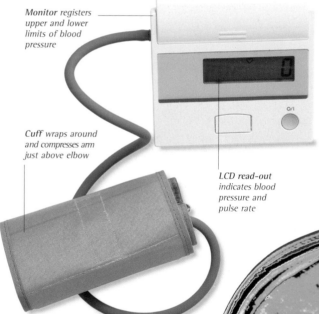

Monitor registers upper and lower limits of blood pressure

Cuff wraps around and compresses arm just above elbow

LCD read-out indicates blood pressure and pulse rate

Tumour in the left side of the brain

### ◄ PREVENTION

Every one of us can use strategies to prevent disease. Healthy eating, plenty of exercise, and, as adults, avoiding smoking and excess alcohol are just a few. But we can also, from time to time, see a doctor for a general health check up. One indicator of general health is blood pressure – the pressure of blood in the arteries – which is measured by using a monitor like this. A person with high blood pressure is at increased risk of serious heart disorders and needs treatment to bring it within a normal range.

e ►►
medicine

Drugs treat symptoms, prevent serious illness, or supply substances that the body lacks

### DIAGNOSIS ►

A doctor carries out a diagnosis to find out what is wrong with a person. First, the doctor asks what symptoms the patient is aware of and also asks about medical history – illnesses that the patient, or sometimes, family members have had in the past. The doctor then looks for signs of disease. Further investigations may include tests on blood or urine, or imaging techniques such as X-rays, MRI, or CT scans. This MRI scan reveals a cancerous tumour in the brain of a woman who had noticed changes in her behaviour.

### DRUG TREATMENT ▲

Drugs are chemicals that affect the way the body works and help us combat disease. Some, such as digitalis drugs for heart problems, were originally derived from plants or other natural sources (in this example, from the foxglove plant) but most are now synthesized artificially. Examples of types of drugs include analgesics, which relieve pain; antibiotics, which kill bacteria; antidepressants, which relieve depression; and vaccines, which prevent infection. Most drugs are potentially harmful and must be taken in recommended doses or as prescribed by a doctor.

X-ray source
*moves around
patient's head*

◄ OPEN SURGERY

Open surgery involves cutting into the body to remove, repair, or replace damaged or abnormal tissues. During surgery the patient is anaesthetized so she or he feels no pain. The operating theatre is scrupulously cleaned. Surgeons, anaesthetists, and nurses wear surgical gloves, caps, face masks, and gowns to maintain sterile conditions and minimize the risk of infecting their patient.

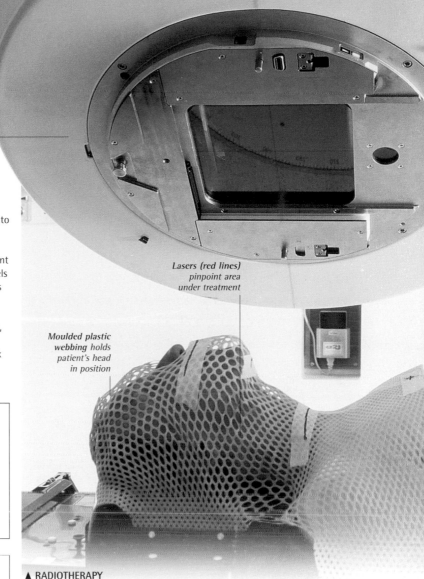

*Lasers (red lines)
pinpoint area
under treatment*

*Moulded plastic
webbing holds
patient's head
in position*

## SPECIALIST SURGERY

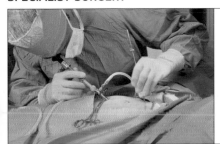

### KEYHOLE SURGERY

In minimally invasive surgery, often called keyhole surgery, a surgeon makes only a very small incision or incisions to repair or remove tissue. As shown left, the surgeon looks inside the body using a viewing tube called an endoscope and introduces fine instruments through the small opening(s) to perform surgery.

### MICROSURGERY

This surgeon is using a binocular microscope to magnify tiny and delicate body structures while he operates on them. Microsurgery is used to reconnect fine nerves or blood vessels, allowing, for example, severed fingers to be reattached. It is also used for operations on tiny structures in the eyes, ears, and reproductive systems.

▲ RADIOTHERAPY

A patient receives radiotherapy as treatment for a cancerous tumour. Radiotherapy uses high-energy radiation generated by a linear accelerator (above, top) to destroy cancer cells with minimal damage to normal cells. Modern machines can penetrate deep into tissues and target a tumour with precise doses of radiation. Radiotherapy is used to treat a range of cancers, often combined with chemotherapy (the use of anticancer drugs) and surgery to remove abnormal tissue.

### LASER SURGERY

A laser uses a high-intensity light beam that generates intense heat to surgically repair damaged tissue by bonding torn edges together, or to destroy damaged or abnormal tissue. Here it is being used to reattach a detached retina – the light-sensitive lining of the eyeball. Lasers are also used to reshape the cornea to correct short-sightedness.

### PHYSIOTHERAPY

This type of treatment uses physical techniques to restore normal body function or improve mobility, strength, or flexibility after illness, surgery, or injury. It is also used to prevent a person becoming immobile during a long-term illness. The techniques include manipulation, exercise, massage, ultrasound, electrical stimulation, and hydrotherapy, where the patient is treated while effectively weightless in a heated pool. Here a physiotherapist manipulates his patient's thigh and back to help relieve her lower back pain.

*Physiotherapist
manipulates
patient's hip*

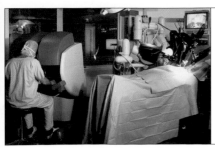

### ROBOTIC SURGERY

A surgeon (left) uses a remotely controlled surgical robot (centre) to perform minimally invasive surgery on a patient's heart through a tiny incision in the chest. The surgeon sits at a console and, looking inside the chest using an endoscope, moves joysticks to manipulate the robotic arms to perform surgical tasks.

# FOOD PROCESSOR

The body needs nutrients for growth, repair, and to provide energy. However, these nutrients are locked and unusable inside the large molecules that make up the food we eat until they can be processed during digestion. The digestive system takes in food, digests (breaks it down) into simple nutrient molecules, and absorbs them so they can be carried in the bloodstream to body cells. It then disposes of any waste. Mechanical digestion in the mouth and stomach uses muscle power to break up food. Chemical digestion is by digesters called enzymes.

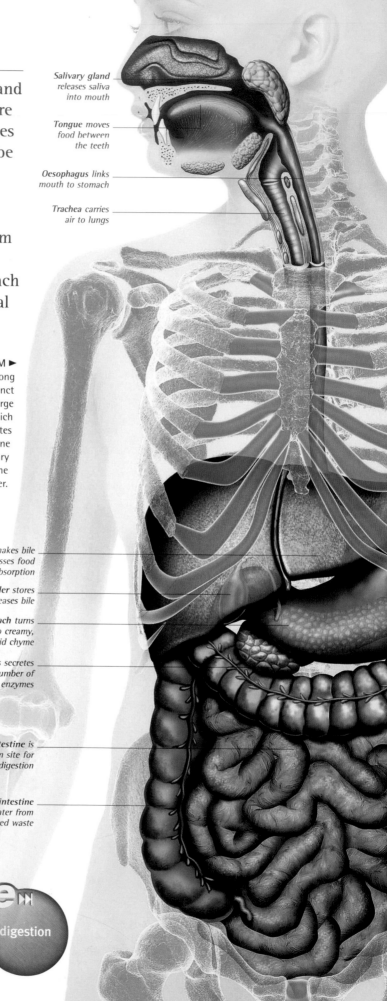

Salivary gland releases saliva into mouth

Tongue moves food between the teeth

Oesophagus links mouth to stomach

Trachea carries air to lungs

## DIGESTIVE SYSTEM ▶

The main part of the digestive system is a 9-m (30-ft) long tube called the alimentary canal, which is divided into distinct regions – oesophagus, stomach, and the small and large intestines. The oesophagus pushes food to the stomach, which stores and partially digests it. The small intestine completes digestion and absorbs its products, while the large intestine disposes of undigested waste. Attached to the alimentary canal are the accessory organs that aid digestion – the tongue, teeth, salivary glands, gall bladder, and liver.

## ENZYME ACTION

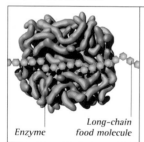

Enzyme | Long-chain food molecule

### ACTIVE SITE
Enzymes are protein catalysts – they speed up the breakdown of complex food molecules, sometimes making it millions of times faster. Each enzyme acts on a particular food molecule; in this case the enzyme is amylase (blue) and the food molecule is starch (orange). Starch attaches itself to a part of the enzyme called its active site.

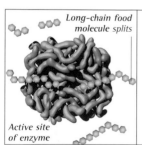

Long-chain food molecule splits

Active site of enzyme

### SPLITTING MOLECULES
Once the food molecule is locked onto the enzyme, the active site changes shape. By adding water molecules, the long chain of the starch molecule is broken into smaller units called sugars. Enzymes in the small intestine lining break down these sub-units further into the simple sugar glucose, which can be absorbed into the bloodstream.

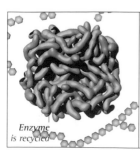

Enzyme is recycled

### RECYCLED ENZYME
Once the reaction is complete and the products of starch breakdown are released, the enzyme is recycled to attract more starch molecules. Digestive enzymes are produced by the salivary glands, stomach, pancreas, and small intestine. Without them the breakdown of food would be so slow that life would be impossible.

Liver makes bile and processes food after absorption

Gall bladder stores and releases bile

Stomach turns food into creamy, liquid chyme

Pancreas secretes a number of digestive enzymes

Small intestine is the main site for food digestion

Large intestine absorbs water from undigested waste

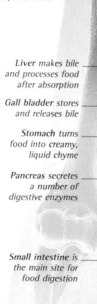

digestion

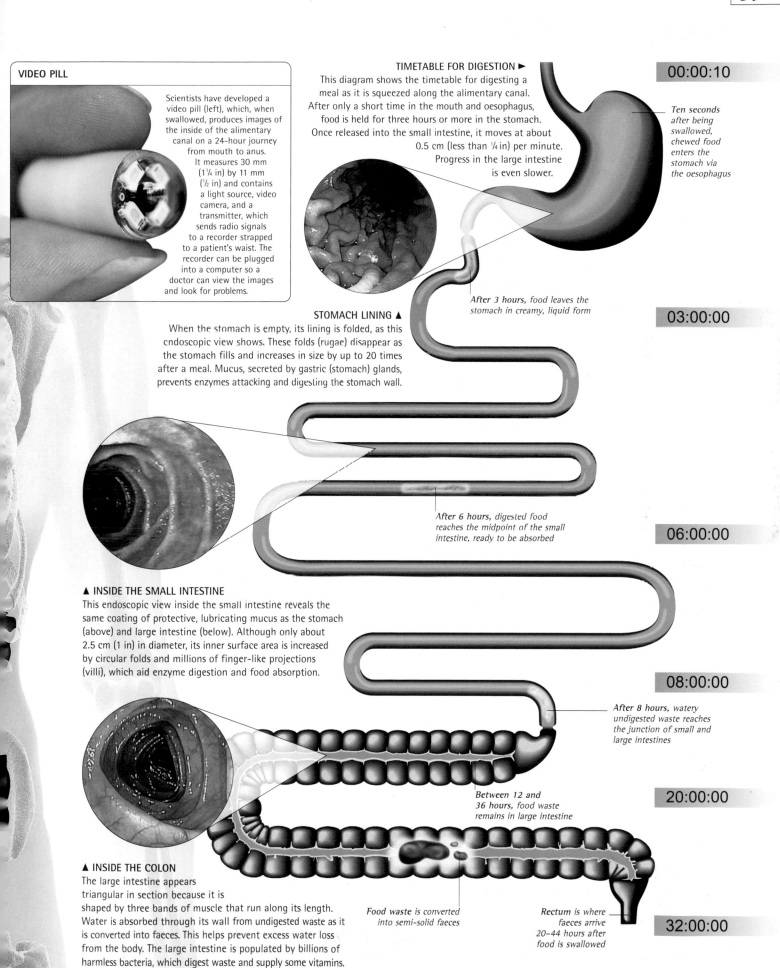

**VIDEO PILL**

Scientists have developed a video pill (left), which, when swallowed, produces images of the inside of the alimentary canal on a 24-hour journey from mouth to anus. It measures 30 mm (1¼ in) by 11 mm (½ in) and contains a light source, video camera, and a transmitter, which sends radio signals to a recorder strapped to a patient's waist. The recorder can be plugged into a computer so a doctor can view the images and look for problems.

**TIMETABLE FOR DIGESTION ►**
This diagram shows the timetable for digesting a meal as it is squeezed along the alimentary canal. After only a short time in the mouth and oesophagus, food is held for three hours or more in the stomach. Once released into the small intestine, it moves at about 0.5 cm (less than ¼ in) per minute. Progress in the large intestine is even slower.

**STOMACH LINING ▲**
When the stomach is empty, its lining is folded, as this endoscopic view shows. These folds (rugae) disappear as the stomach fills and increases in size by up to 20 times after a meal. Mucus, secreted by gastric (stomach) glands, prevents enzymes attacking and digesting the stomach wall.

**▲ INSIDE THE SMALL INTESTINE**
This endoscopic view inside the small intestine reveals the same coating of protective, lubricating mucus as the stomach (above) and large intestine (below). Although only about 2.5 cm (1 in) in diameter, its inner surface area is increased by circular folds and millions of finger-like projections (villi), which aid enzyme digestion and food absorption.

**▲ INSIDE THE COLON**
The large intestine appears triangular in section because it is shaped by three bands of muscle that run along its length. Water is absorbed through its wall from undigested waste as it is converted into faeces. This helps prevent excess water loss from the body. The large intestine is populated by billions of harmless bacteria, which digest waste and supply some vitamins.

*Ten seconds after being swallowed, chewed food enters the stomach via the oesophagus*

*After 3 hours, food leaves the stomach in creamy, liquid form*

*After 6 hours, digested food reaches the midpoint of the small intestine, ready to be absorbed*

*After 8 hours, watery undigested waste reaches the junction of small and large intestines*

*Between 12 and 36 hours, food waste remains in large intestine*

*Food waste is converted into semi-solid faeces*

*Rectum is where faeces arrive 20–44 hours after food is swallowed*

00:00:10

03:00:00

06:00:00

08:00:00

20:00:00

32:00:00

# TEETH AND SWALLOWING

The hardest organs in the body are our teeth, embedded in the
upper and lower jaws. Teeth cut, chew, and crush the food we eat
into small pieces so they become easy to swallow
and can be digested efficiently. Humans have
two sets of teeth during their lifetime.
The first set of 20 milk teeth is
replaced by 32 permanent adult teeth
during childhood and the teenage
years. Swallowing food has three
separate stages. The first stage, in
the mouth, is under conscious
control, while swallowing by
the throat and oesophagus are
automatic, reflex actions.

**FULL SET OF TEETH ▶**
The 32 teeth, 16 in each jaw, in a full set of adult
teeth vary in shape and function. In each jaw there
are four incisors, two canines, four premolars, and six
molars. (The rear molars – the wisdom teeth – have
been removed here). Flat, chisel-like incisors slice food
up into manageable pieces. Pointed canines grip,
pierce, and tear food. Premolar teeth, with broad
crowns and two raised edges or cusps, crush and chew
food. Molar teeth with even broader crowns
and four cusps bite with great force
to grind food into a paste.

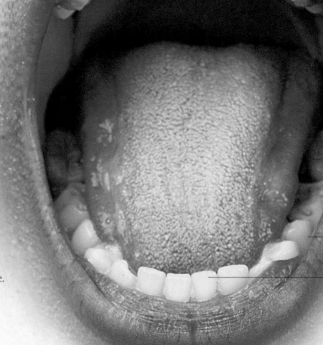

*Canine is cone-shaped with a pointed tip*

*Molar is large flat tooth with a double root*

*Premolar has double cusps*

*Incisor has a sharp cutting edge*

## CHEWING AND SWALLOWING

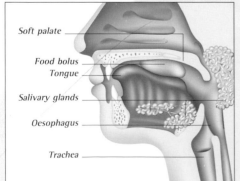

Soft palate / Food bolus / Tongue / Salivary glands / Oesophagus / Trachea

**MOUTH**
Food is chewed into tiny pieces, which are glued
together by slimy mucus in saliva to form a slippery
ball called a bolus. When we are ready to swallow, the
muscular tongue pushes the bolus against the roof of
the mouth and back towards the throat. The soft palate
flaps upwards to stop food going up into the nasal cavity.

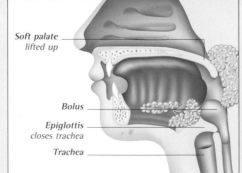

Soft palate lifted up / Bolus / Epiglottis closes trachea / Trachea

**THROAT**
The next two stages of swallowing are under automatic
control. When the food bolus touches the back of the
throat, it triggers a reflex action. Muscular contractions
push the bolus down the throat and into the oesophagus.
Breathing stops briefly, and the epiglottis seals off the
trachea to stop food "going down the wrong way".

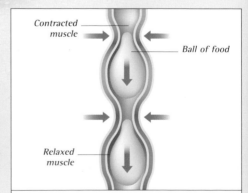

Contracted muscle / Ball of food / Relaxed muscle

**OESOPHAGUS**
In the final stage of swallowing, food is moved from the
throat to the stomach by peristalsis – waves of contraction
of smooth muscles in the wall of the oesophagus. Muscle
behind the bolus contracts while muscle around and in
front of the bolus relaxes. This pushes the bolus downwards,
much as finger pressure squeezes toothpaste out of a tube.

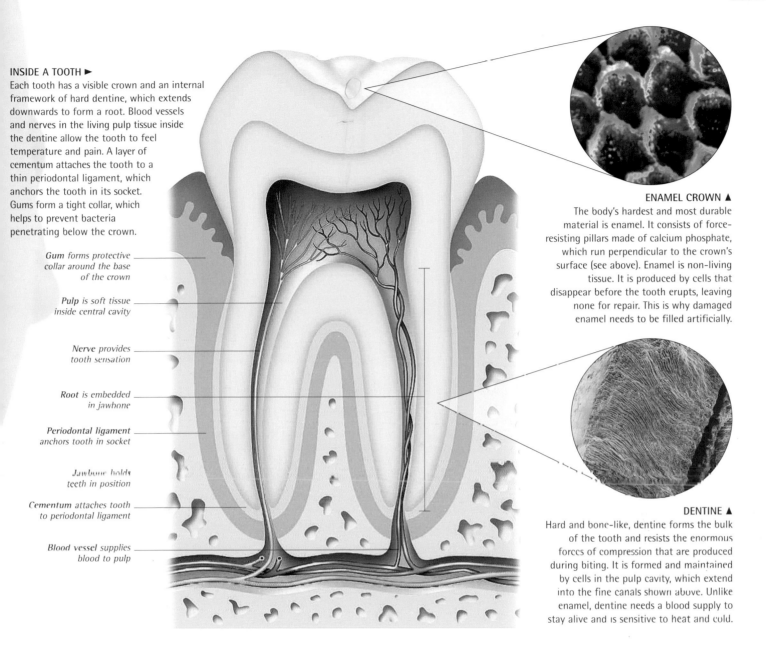

## INSIDE A TOOTH ▶

Each tooth has a visible crown and an internal framework of hard dentine, which extends downwards to form a root. Blood vessels and nerves in the living pulp tissue inside the dentine allow the tooth to feel temperature and pain. A layer of cementum attaches the tooth to a thin periodontal ligament, which anchors the tooth in its socket. Gums form a tight collar, which helps to prevent bacteria penetrating below the crown.

*Gum* forms protective collar around the base of the crown

*Pulp* is soft tissue inside central cavity

*Nerve* provides tooth sensation

*Root* is embedded in jawbone

*Periodontal ligament* anchors tooth in socket

*Jawbone* holds teeth in position

*Cementum* attaches tooth to periodontal ligament

*Blood vessel* supplies blood to pulp

### ENAMEL CROWN ▲
The body's hardest and most durable material is enamel. It consists of force-resisting pillars made of calcium phosphate, which run perpendicular to the crown's surface (see above). Enamel is non-living tissue. It is produced by cells that disappear before the tooth erupts, leaving none for repair. This is why damaged enamel needs to be filled artificially.

### DENTINE ▲
Hard and bone-like, dentine forms the bulk of the tooth and resists the enormous forces of compression that are produced during biting. It is formed and maintained by cells in the pulp cavity, which extend into the fine canals shown above. Unlike enamel, dentine needs a blood supply to stay alive and is sensitive to heat and cold.

## HOW TEETH DECAY

**PLAQUE**
Stuck on the surface of this magnified tooth is plaque (yellow), a mixture of food remains and bacteria. Plaque builds up on teeth if they are not brushed regularly. Once it starts to accumulate, it is hard to shift because the bacteria in plaque produce a sticky "glue" to hold them in place. If it is not removed, plaque can lead to tooth decay.

**BACTERIA**
These plaque bacteria feed on the sugars in plaque and release acid waste which, over time, dissolves enamel and leads to dental decay. As decay reaches the dentine and sensitive pulp, it causes pain and eventually kills pulp cells so that the tooth becomes rotten. Plaque build-up and tooth decay can be prevented by regular brushing and flossing.

## IMPROVING APPEARANCE

A common sight in teenagers, braces alter and improve the appearance of permanent teeth that do not line up properly. Braces are fitted by specialist dentists called orthodontists. A brace consists of ceramic or metal brackets, each attached to a tooth. An arch wire connects and applies pressure via the brackets, gradually moving the teeth into their new positions. As the teeth move, the jawbone remodels itself around their roots so they stay in place.

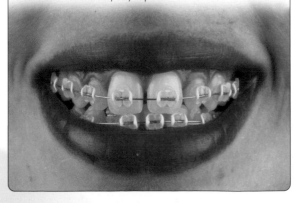

# DIGESTION AND ABSORPTION

To be turned into simple nutrients that can be used by the body, food is moved through the stomach and intestines by waves of muscular contraction, called peristalsis and digested by mechanical churning and enzymes. Digestion takes place primarily in the stomach and small intestine, while absorption occurs in the small intestine and undigested waste is disposed of by the large intestine. Water released into the gut during digestion is mostly reabsorbed to prevent dehydration.

**FROM STOMACH TO COLON ▶**
In the stomach, muscular contraction and gastric juice turn chewed food into a creamy liquid that is released into the small intestine. Here, bile and enzymes break it down into glucose, amino acids, fatty acids, and other nutrients. These are absorbed through the small intestine wall into the bloodstream. Undigested waste travels along the colon where it is dried out and passed out from the rectum as faeces.

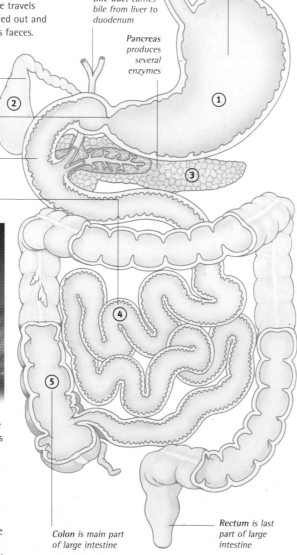

*Oesophagus moves food from throat*

*Bolus is ball of chewed food*

*Stomach partly digests food*

*Bile duct carries bile from liver to duodenum*

*Pancreas produces several enzymes*

*Gall bladder stores bile*

*Pyloric sphincter is ring of muscle*

*Duodenum is first part of small intestine*

*Small intestine is longest part of gut*

*Colon is main part of large intestine*

*Rectum is last part of large intestine*

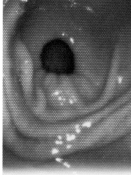

**▲ PYLORIC SPHINCTER**
A sphincter is a ring of muscle that opens (contracts) or closes (relaxes) to control the flow of substances. This endoscopic view looks from the stomach through the partially relaxed pyloric sphincter into the duodenum beyond. The sphincter guards the exit of the stomach, controlling the flow of partially digested food called chyme into the duodenum.

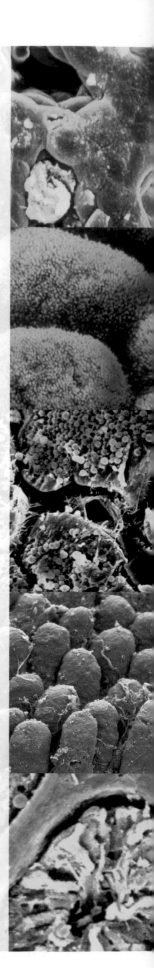

**① STOMACH**
This magnified view of the epithelium that lines the stomach shows openings that lead to gastric pits. These pits contain gastric glands, which secrete highly acid gastric juice containing hydrochloric acid and pepsin, an enzyme that digests proteins. The glands also produce protective mucus, which coats the stomach lining and prevents gastric juice from digesting the lining itself.

**② GALL BLADDER**
Tucked behind the liver, the gall bladder is a small muscular bag that stores, concentrates, and releases bile. A greenish liquid made by the liver, bile is concentrated by epithelial cells in the gall bladder lining (right). When food arrives from the stomach, the muscular walls of the gall bladder contract to squirt bile into the duodenum where it breaks down fats, making them easier to digest.

**③ PANCREAS**
These clusters of cells in the pancreas, called acinar cells, produce daily around 2 litres (3½ pt) of digestive pancreatic juice, which travels along a duct to the duodenum. The enzymes in pancreatic juice digest starch, proteins, and – aided by bile – fats in the small intestine. Other cells in the pancreas release the hormones insulin and glucagon into the bloodstream.

**④ SMALL INTESTINE**
Around 6-m (20-ft) long, the small intestine's inner surface area is greatly increased by a carpet of microscopic villi (right). Digestive enzymes on the surface of the villi, and those from the pancreas, complete the digestion of food into its simplest components. These include glucose and amino acids, which are absorbed through the villi and released back into the bloodstream.

**⑤ COLON**
The large intestine is some 1.5 m (5 ft) long, and is so named because it is much wider than the small intestine. The major part of the large intestine, the colon, has tubular glands (yellow) in its wall, which are shown in cross-section on the right. The glands secrete mucus, and also absorb water from the liquid waste that flows along the colon. This turns the waste into semi-solid faeces.

## HOW THE STOMACH FILLS AND EMPTIES

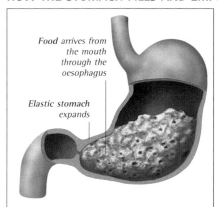

**FILLING UP**
The thought, smell, sight, and taste of food all stimulate glands in the stomach wall to release gastric juice ready to receive chewed food from the oesophagus. When food arrives, it can expand the stomach to 20 times its normal size. Waves of muscle contractions help to mix it with gastric juice.

*Food arrives from the mouth through the oesophagus*

*Elastic stomach expands*

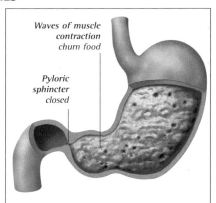

**DIGESTION**
With the pyloric sphincter closed, peristaltic waves increase in intensity to churn the food into a creamy liquid called chyme. Secretion of gastric juice continues, with the enzyme pepsin digesting proteins present in food. These processes are controlled by the nervous and endocrine systems.

*Waves of muscle contraction churn food*

*Pyloric sphincter closed*

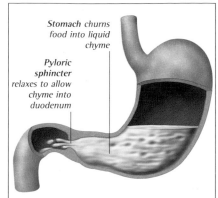

**EMPTYING**
Food is held in the stomach for three to four hours then released steadily into the duodenum to give the small intestine time to digest it. The stomach's muscular wall contracts, pushing chyme against the pyloric sphincter. The sphincter relaxes to allow small amounts to flow into the duodenum.

*Stomach churns food into liquid chyme*

*Pyloric sphincter relaxes to allow chyme into duodenum*

### WATER RELEASED DURING DIGESTION

This table shows the large amounts of water that are released in digestive juices and bile during digestion. Almost all of it is reabsorbed and returned to the bloodstream to help maintain the body's water balance (*see also* water balance table, p.75).

| WATER INTO GUT | | WATER LOST | |
|---|---|---|---|
| Saliva | 1 litre (1¾ pt) | In faeces | 0.1 litre (⅛ pt) |
| Bile | 1 litre (1¾ pt) | | |
| Gastric juice | 2 litres (3½ pt) | | |
| Pancreatic juice | 2 litres (3½ pt) | | |
| Intestinal juice | 1 litre (1¾ pt) | | |
| Total | 7 litres (12¼ pt) | | |
| Water reabsorbed from small and large intestine | 98.5 per cent | | |

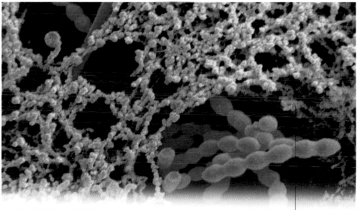

**▲ HARMLESS BACTERIA**
The billions of bacteria that colonize the lining of the colon are mostly harmless and even beneficial and include *Lactobacillus* (yellow) and *Streptococcus* (blue). They feed on undigested waste arriving from the small intestine, yielding the gas that creates wind, as well as B complex and K vitamins, which are absorbed through the colon wall and used by the body. Bacteria are constantly lost, making up to 50 per cent of faeces.

*Lactobacillus is one type of colon bacteria*

*Rod-shaped Salmonella bacteria multiply in undercooked chicken*

digestion

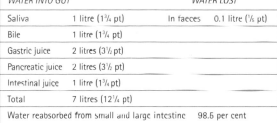

**◄ HARMFUL BACTERIA**
The food and drinks we consume often contain bacteria, most of which are destroyed by acidic gastric juice in the stomach. Among those that can survive the acid bath is the bacterium *Salmonella*. It releases toxins (poisons) that affect the small intestine, causing severe vomiting and diarrhoea. The source of *Salmonella* is contaminated food, especially chicken and eggs. Infection leaves a person weak, dehydrated, and in need of rest and plenty of fluids.

# NUTRITION AND ENERGY

Food provides the nutrients we need to build and maintain our bodies, and to supply them with energy. Carbohydrates, proteins, and fats make up most of our diet, and essential vitamins and minerals are needed in small amounts. To remain healthy, and at the right weight for our height, we need a broad mixture of foods, eaten in the right amounts. A balanced diet should contain about 55 per cent carbohydrate, 15 per cent protein, and 30 per cent fat, and provide the right amount of energy for normal activity. People who regularly eat more than they need become overweight or even obese.

nutrition

*Carrots are rich in vitamin A*

*Courgettes have a high water content*

*Wholegrain rice releases its energy slowly*

*Bran cereal is rich in fibre*

**FRUIT AND JUICES**
Fruit, such as oranges and apples, contain a range of vitamins and minerals. Their sweetness comes from simple sugars, a ready source of energy. They are rich sources of water and dietary fibre, the indigestible plant material that adds bulk to food and aids movement through the intestines.

**VEGETABLES**
Rich in complex and simple carbohydrates, and also in water and dietary fibre, vegetables such as fresh carrots and yellow peppers are a key source of vitamins and minerals. Some, such as broccoli, contain anti-oxidants – substances that reduce the risk of cancers or heart disease developing. Five portions of either fruit or vegetables should be eaten each day (see box).

**COMPLEX CARBOHYDRATES**
Cereals, rice, potatoes, pasta, and bread are all sources of the complex carbohydrate starch, which provides a slow-release source of glucose – the body's main fuel – when digested. These foods also contain fibre and minerals, such as iron and calcium, and B group vitamins. Foods containing complex carbohydrates should form the bulk of a balanced diet.

## MAKING BODY FUELS FROM FOOD

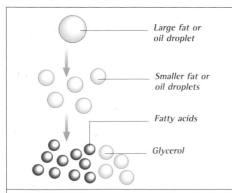

*Large fat or oil droplet*

*Smaller fat or oil droplets*

*Fatty acids*

*Glycerol*

**FAT-RICH FOODS**
Fats and oils from animal and vegetable sources are emulsified in the small intestine into small droplets by bile. These are then broken down by enzymes into glycerol and fatty acids, which are used by the body as an important source of energy, to build cell components, and for storage and insulation as fat.

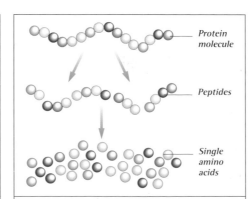

*Protein molecule*

*Peptides*

*Single amino acids*

**PROTEINS**
Long-chain protein molecules from meat, fish, and other sources are broken down in the stomach and small intestine, first into shorter peptides, and then into single amino acids. Inside the body, the 20 types of amino acid are reassembled into many different kinds of proteins, including structural proteins, antibodies, and enzymes.

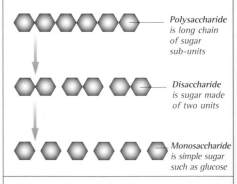

*Polysaccharide is long chain of sugar sub-units*

*Disaccharide is sugar made of two units*

*Monosaccharide is simple sugar such as glucose*

**CARBOHYDRATES**
The main complex carbohydrate in the diet is starch from plant sources, which consists of long chains of sugar sub-units. These are broken down, mainly in the small intestine, into disaccharides (two units) and then monosaccharides – simple sugars such as glucose, which provide the body with its main energy source.

## CALORIES PER DAY

Calories per day (y-axis: 0, 500, 1,000, 1,500, 2,000, 2,500, 3,000)

Bar chart categories:
- Infant (9–12 months old)
- Child (8 years old)
- Boy (15 years old)
- Girl (15 years old)
- Man (30 years old – active)
- Woman (30 years old – active)
- Man (30 years old – inactive)
- Woman (30 years old – inactive)
- Woman (30 years old – breast-feeding)

◀ CALORIES PER DAY

Each of us has our own daily energy requirement from food, measured in calories (kcal), although scientists use units called kilojoules (kJ) – 1 kcal = 4.187 kJ. The graph on the left shows that on average, men need more energy than women, because they are bigger. Breast-feeding and pregnant women need more energy to provide for their babies, and teenagers require extra energy while they are growing.

*Milk provides calcium for bone and tooth growth*

### ESSENTIAL FATTY ACIDS

Most of the fatty acids we need for processes such as skin repair and a healthy immune system are produced by the body. Those that are not have to be absorbed from food. They are called essential fatty acids (EFAs) and are vital to health. EFAs are found in vegetable oils, oily fish, and some nuts. Cod liver oil (in capsules, right) contains an EFA that improves nerve function and is thought to be important for brain development.

*Cakes are rich in fat and sugar*

### PROTEIN-RICH FOODS

Protein-rich foods, such as meat, eggs, fish, and beans, provide the raw materials for the body's growth and repair. They form a vital part of the diet but should be eaten in moderation because most contain fats. However, oily fish provide fatty acids, which are beneficial to health.

### DAIRY FOODS

Milk and products made from animal milk, such as butter, cheese, and yoghurt, are good sources of the mineral calcium. They contain variable amounts of protein, but also fat. Butter, for example, is up to 70 per cent fat, and should be eaten in small amounts. To keep fat levels at recommended levels, it is better to consume lower-fat dairy foods, such as semi-skimmed milk.

### FAT AND SUGAR

Fatty and sugary foods such as cakes, biscuits, and sweets, as well as foods such as crisps that are high in fat and salt, are best eaten infrequently and in small quantities. They provide plenty of energy, but often too much fat (and in some cases salt) but little else of nutritional value, such as vitamins or minerals.

◀ OBESITY EPIDEMIC

Obesity is on the increase. In the Western world, growing numbers of children and adults are at least 20 per cent heavier than they should be for their height. Excess body fat accumulates when people regularly eat more calories than can be used by their bodies. Obesity has become common because people are less active than in former times and eat more calorie-laden, processed foods. Obesity greatly increases the risk of heart disease, high blood pressure, diabetes, and some cancers. The remedy is to increase daily exercise and to eat fresh foods, especially fruit, vegetables, and oily fish.

### FIVE A DAY

The World Health Organization recommends that we eat five portions of fruit or vegetables daily to help reduce the risk of developing cancer and coronary heart disease, which together cause 60 per cent of all deaths. One portion could be half a grapefruit, an apple, or a bowl of salad. A glass of pure fruit juice is also a portion, but it only supplies the vitamins, not the fibre, of fresh fruit.

# BREATHING SYSTEM

The role of the breathing, or respiratory, system is to get oxygen into the body and to remove carbon dioxide. Oxygen is required by the trillions of body cells to release the energy they need to live. Cells cannot store oxygen, so they need a constant supply. Carbon dioxide is the waste product of energy release and would poison the body if it were not removed continuously. The main parts of the breathing system are the lungs, through which oxygen enters the bloodstream, and the air passages that carry air to and from the lungs.

**▲ UP THE NOSE**

This CT scan shows in 3-D the three bony plates, or conchae, on each side of the nasal cavity. Cold, dry, and dirty air would damage the lungs, so the mucous membrane covering the conchae warms and moistens the breathed-in air as it flows over them. Mucus covering the membrane traps dirt particles and disease-causing pathogens.

**RESPIRATORY SYSTEM ▶**

The respiratory system is located in the head, neck, and chest and consists of the lungs and air passages that carry air to and from the lungs. When air is breathed in, it passes along the nose, throat, larynx, trachea, and then into a bronchus, which enters a lung. Inside the lung, bronchi divide repeatedly, ending as tiny alveoli through which oxygen enters the blood. Breathed-out air moves in the reverse direction.

*Larynx (voice box)*

*Ribs surround and protect lungs*

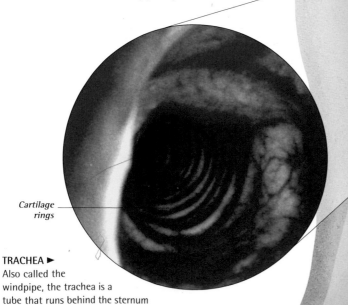

*Cartilage rings*

**TRACHEA ▶**

Also called the windpipe, the trachea is a tube that runs behind the sternum and carries air between the larynx and lungs. At its lower end, the trachea splits into two branches called bronchi, which enter the lungs. The trachea is reinforced by 20 C-shaped pieces of cartilage, as this view through a bronchoscope shows. These rings stop the trachea collapsing inwards when air is breathed in. The lining of the trachea produces a sticky mucus that traps dust and pathogens.

## ◄ BRONCHIAL TREE

This cast shows the network of air passages in the two lungs. The trachea descends through the chest and divides into two main bronchi – serving the left and right lungs. Each main bronchus divides into smaller bronchi, which branch repeatedly to yet narrower branches called bronchioles. This complex structure is often called a bronchial tree because, turned upside down, it resembles a tree in which the trachea is the trunk, the bronchi its branches, and the bronchioles, twigs.

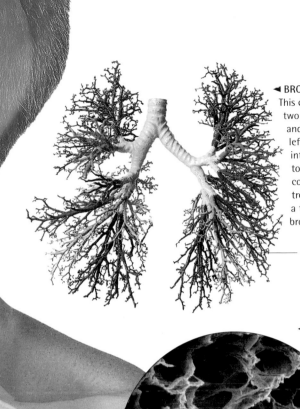

*Resin cast of branching network inside lung*

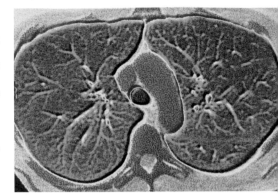

## ▲ INSIDE THE CHEST

A CT scan of a "slice" through the chest reveals how much space the lungs (dark blue) occupy. The paler blue lines within the lungs are the bronchi. The front of the body is at the top, and the backbone can be seen at the bottom. The ribs surrounding the lungs are also evident. The blue circle (centre) is the trachea, next to which is the aortic arch (dark orange oval) and superior vena cava (dark orange circle).

## ◄ BRONCHIOLE AND ALVEOLI

This magnified section through lung tissue shows some of the 150 million alveoli that fill much of each lung and give it its spongy texture. Blind-ended alveoli are tiny air sacs through which oxygen is taken into the bloodstream and carbon dioxide is expelled. Each group of alveoli is located at the end of a bronchiole (left, with ruffled edge). Bronchioles are the finest of all air passages and penetrate deep into the lungs

breathing

*Bronchus is a branch of the trachea*

*Bronchiole is a fine branch of a bronchus*

*Diaphragm is a sheet of muscle*

## PROTECTING THE LUNGS

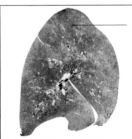

*Alveolar macrophage*

*Dust particle being engulfed*

### DUST CELLS
This magnified view inside an alveolus shows two dust cells, or alveolar macrophages. The job of dust cells is to surround and engulf infectious micro-organisms or dust particles that reach the alveoli to stop them interfering with gas exchange. One of the dust cells shown here has elongated to surround a dust particle.

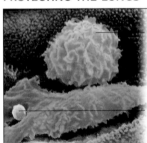

*Section through whole healthy lung*

### HEALTHY LUNG
A healthy lung appears pink in colour because of the large numbers of blood vessels inside it. Dust and other pollutants in air are mostly filtered out by cilia and mucus in the nose, trachea, and bronchi before they reach the lung tissue. However, city dwellers breathe in more particles than people who live in the country.

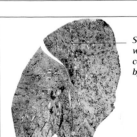

*Section through whole lung contaminated by tar*

### CONTAMINATED LUNG
This lung tissue belonged to a heavy smoker. Tars in cigarette smoke condense in the lungs over many years to leave this discoloration. These tars contain many carcinogens, substances that can cause cancer. Substances in tars and cigarette smoke also destroy dust cells, so that particles gather in, and damage, the alveoli.

# GETTING OXYGEN

Cells constantly consume oxygen and release waste carbon dioxide as they obtain energy from glucose during cell respiration. Oxygen is supplied from air breathed in by the lungs and is carried by the blood to tissue cells. Carbon dioxide is carried by the blood from tissue cells to the lungs to be breathed out. The swapping of oxygen for carbon dioxide in both lungs and tissues is called gas exchange. Breathing movements are produced by the action of the diaphragm and the intercostal muscles in the thorax.

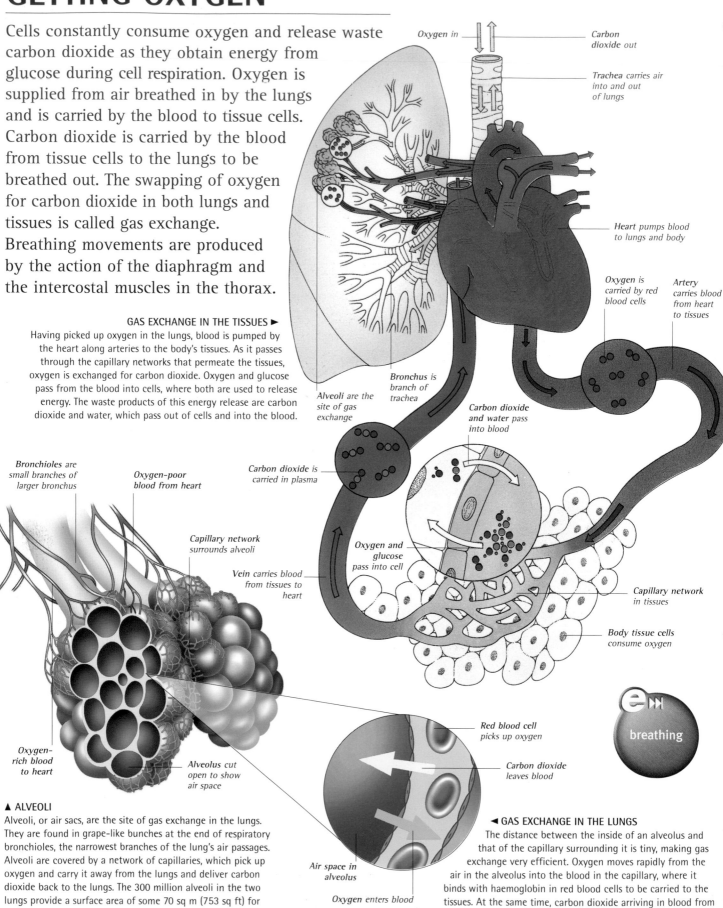

*Oxygen in*

*Carbon dioxide out*

*Trachea carries air into and out of lungs*

*Heart pumps blood to lungs and body*

*Oxygen is carried by red blood cells*

*Artery carries blood from heart to tissues*

*Bronchus is branch of trachea*

*Alveoli are the site of gas exchange*

*Carbon dioxide and water pass into blood*

**GAS EXCHANGE IN THE TISSUES ▶**
Having picked up oxygen in the lungs, blood is pumped by the heart along arteries to the body's tissues. As it passes through the capillary networks that permeate the tissues, oxygen is exchanged for carbon dioxide. Oxygen and glucose pass from the blood into cells, where both are used to release energy. The waste products of this energy release are carbon dioxide and water, which pass out of cells and into the blood.

*Carbon dioxide is carried in plasma*

*Oxygen and glucose pass into cell*

*Capillary network in tissues*

*Body tissue cells consume oxygen*

*Bronchioles are small branches of larger bronchus*

*Oxygen-poor blood from heart*

*Capillary network surrounds alveoli*

*Vein carries blood from tissues to heart*

*Oxygen-rich blood to heart*

*Alveolus cut open to show air space*

*Red blood cell picks up oxygen*

*Carbon dioxide leaves blood*

breathing

**▲ ALVEOLI**
Alveoli, or air sacs, are the site of gas exchange in the lungs. They are found in grape-like bunches at the end of respiratory bronchioles, the narrowest branches of the lung's air passages. Alveoli are covered by a network of capillaries, which pick up oxygen and carry it away from the lungs and deliver carbon dioxide back to the lungs. The 300 million alveoli in the two lungs provide a surface area of some 70 sq m (753 sq ft) for taking in oxygen – about 35 times the surface area of the skin.

*Air space in alveolus*

*Oxygen enters blood*

**◀ GAS EXCHANGE IN THE LUNGS**
The distance between the inside of an alveolus and that of the capillary surrounding it is tiny, making gas exchange very efficient. Oxygen moves rapidly from the air in the alveolus into the blood in the capillary, where it binds with haemoglobin in red blood cells to be carried to the tissues. At the same time, carbon dioxide arriving in blood from the tissues moves swiftly into the alveolus and is breathed out.

# BREATHING IN – BREATHING OUT

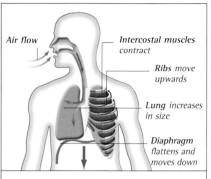

**INHALING**
As we breathe in, or inhale, the diaphragm contracts and flattens and the external intercostal muscles contract, pulling the ribs up and out. This creates space inside the thorax, which causes the elastic lungs to expand. The air pressure inside them is now less than that outside the body, so air is sucked in.

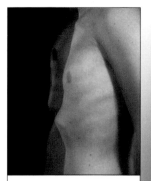

**CHANGE IN CONTOUR**
A double image shows a man's chest rising and falling as he breathes in and out. During quiet breathing, the diaphragm does most of the work so the abdomen moves in and out.

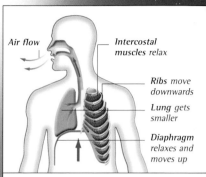

**EXHALING**
As we exhale, or breathe out, the diaphragm relaxes and becomes dome-shaped. The external intercostal muscles relax, so the ribs move downwards and inwards. This reduces space inside the thorax, which makes the lungs shrink. The air pressure inside them is now greater than outside, so air is pushed out.

## COMPARING INHALED AND EXHALED AIR

The proportions of gases in inhaled and exhaled air show how much oxygen the body uses.

| GAS | PERCENTAGE IN INHALED AIR | PERCENTAGE IN EXHALED AIR |
|---|---|---|
| Nitrogen | 78.6 | 78.6 |
| Oxygen | 20.8 | 15.6 |
| Carbon dioxide | 0.04 | 4.0 |
| Water vapour | 0.56 | 1.8 |
| Total | 100 | 100 |

**FREE DIVING ▶**
Humans cannot breathe underwater but divers have overcome this obstacle by breathing air from tanks strapped to their back. Nevertheless, some free divers dive to considerable depths without using air tanks. They practise holding their breath so they can stay underwater for as long as possible. The deeper they dive, the greater the pressure, and the smaller their lungs become. Their heart rate also decreases, sometimes to as low as 50 beats per minute or less.

# EFFECTS OF ASTHMA

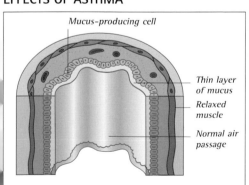

**BETWEEN ATTACKS**
Asthma is a disorder that affects the bronchi and bronchioles in the lungs. People with asthma have intermittent attacks of wheezing and feeling breathless. This diagram shows a section through a bronchiole between asthma attacks. The epithelial lining secretes mucus, while a muscle layer below contracts or relaxes to alter the diameter of the bronchiole.

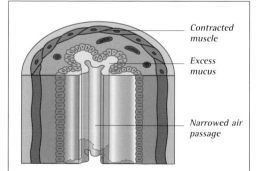

**DURING AN ASTHMA ATTACK**
An asthma attack occurs when muscle in the bronchiole wall contracts to make the air passage very narrow, reducing the amount of air entering the lungs. The bronchiole lining also becomes inflamed and secretes excessive mucus, narrowing the airway still further. Asthma can be triggered by an allergy to, for example, pollen or house dust, or by other factors.

**INHALERS**
This boy is using an inhaler to ease symptoms of breathlessness during an asthma attack. The inhaler delivers a small dose of a bronchodilator drug. When the drug is breathed into the lungs, it relaxes the muscles that narrow the airways. This lets more air into the lungs and makes breathing easier.

# COMMUNICATION

As social animals, we have to communicate to co-exist and survive. Communication allows us to pass on our thoughts and feelings, recall past events, keep track of the present, predict what might happen in the future, and pass on knowledge from one generation to the next. While we live in an age of complex telecommunication, we still use the same forms of face-to-face communication as our distant ancestors. Spoken language, which is unique to humans, allows us to pass on an unlimited range of ideas. Our facial expressions and body language show, often unknowingly, how we are feeling. All types of communication are controlled by the brain.

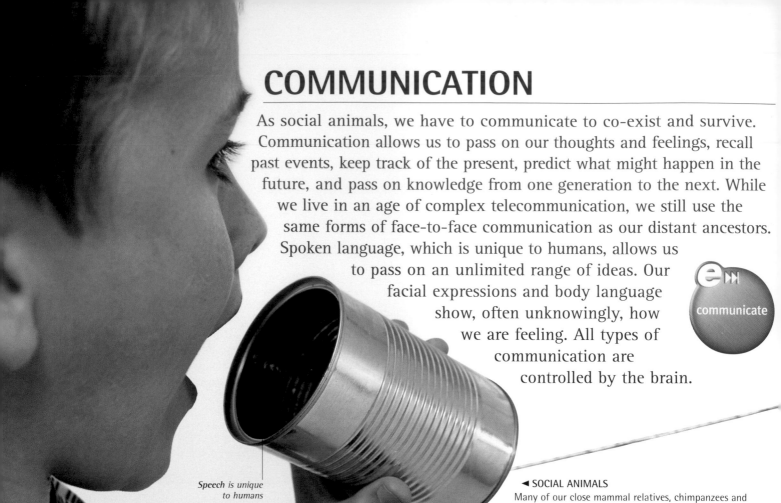

*Speech is unique to humans*

**◄ SOCIAL ANIMALS**
Many of our close mammal relatives, chimpanzees and howler monkeys, for example, are social animals, able to communicate in a number of ways to maintain their social group. But none has the range or intelligence of human social interaction and communication. We are able to use and record spoken and written language – an ability that has enabled us to make extraordinary cultural and technological advances over the past 10,000 years.

**MAKING SOUNDS ►**
To make sounds, the vocal cords, which stretch horizontally across the larynx, are pulled taut as controlled bursts of air are breathed through them from the lungs. This makes the vocal cords vibrate, producing sounds. Under the control of the brain, these sounds are modified by the lips and tongue to produce speech.

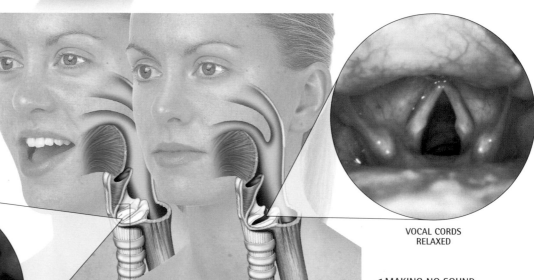

VOCAL CORDS
RELAXED

**◄ MAKING NO SOUND**
When a person is not producing vocal sounds, normal breathing resumes. The vocal cords relax and open to allow the free passage of air to and from the lungs through the larynx and trachea. When men speak, they produce lower-pitched sounds than women because their vocal cords are longer and thicker and vibrate more slowly.

*Larynx contains the vocal cords*

*Trachea carries air to and from lungs*

*Oesophagus carries food to the stomach*

VOCAL CORDS TAUT

## SIGN LANGUAGE

Many hearing-impaired people, who are unable to hear spoken language clearly or at all, use sign language to communicate with each other and with hearing friends and family. Instead of sounds, sign language uses finger, hand, arm, and body movements, hand shapes, lip patterns, and facial expressions to express meanings and ideas. Sign language is not international – like spoken language, it varies from one region to the next. The sign, shown left, is for the letter "r" in the British sign language alphabet.

Sign language is also used in certain situations by people who can hear. Scuba divers sign to each other underwater because speech is not possible, and technicians in TV recording studios use signs when silence is important.

*Despair indicated by arms raised, body slouched*

## ◄ BODY LANGUAGE

The despair of this soccer player at a missed goal – and that of his team's supporters – is all too obvious from their body language. This form of communication uses gestures, posture, and facial expressions that are every bit as revealing as words. More subtle body language can reveal if people are, for example, bored or interested, anxious or confident, or even if they are telling a lie. But some people are better than others at picking up the clues.

## THE BRAIN AND COMMUNICATION

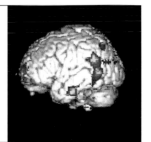

### WHAT DOES IT MEAN?
Like other body activities, speaking and listening are controlled by the brain. Modern technology in the form of PET scans enables scientists to see which parts of the brain "light up" (orange/red) at different stages of speaking and listening. Here areas of the temporal lobe are active as a person works out the meaning of unfamiliar words.

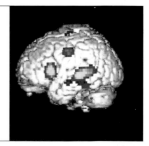

### REPEATING WORDS
This person is repeating words aloud – a brain activity involving Broca's area (bottom left) and a motor area (top centre). Both generate speech, including the co-ordinated movements of the larynx and tongue. Also lit up and active is Wernicke's area (bottom right), which monitors the words being spoken and interprets them.

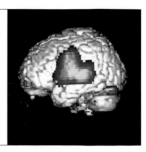

### LISTENING
In this final PET scan, the person is listening to someone talking, without speaking herself. The auditory (hearing) area of the brain lights up as it interprets incoming nerve impulses from the ears. Although speech production occurs only on the left side of the brain, auditory activity occurs on both sides.

## ▲ FACIAL EXPRESSIONS

Humans have a wide range of facial expressions that reflect their feelings and emotions. An expression may be obvious, such as a beaming smile, or more subtle, such as a slightly raised eyebrow. Expressions are produced by more than 30 small muscles. These are attached at one end to the skull and at the other end to small areas of facial skin, which they pull on when they contract. Most facial muscles work in pairs but some, such as the muscles that close the eyes, can be used individually to produce a wink.

*Smiling uses muscles around the eyes as well as the mouth*

# CHEMICAL FACTORIES

Cells resemble chemical factories because thousands of reactions take place inside them. Metabolism describes the chemical processes that both release energy, and construct and repair cells. Nutrients that are absorbed following digestion are processed by the liver, then metabolized by body cells. The heat released by metabolism helps maintain body temperature at 37°C (98.6°F) – the optimal temperature for cell activity.

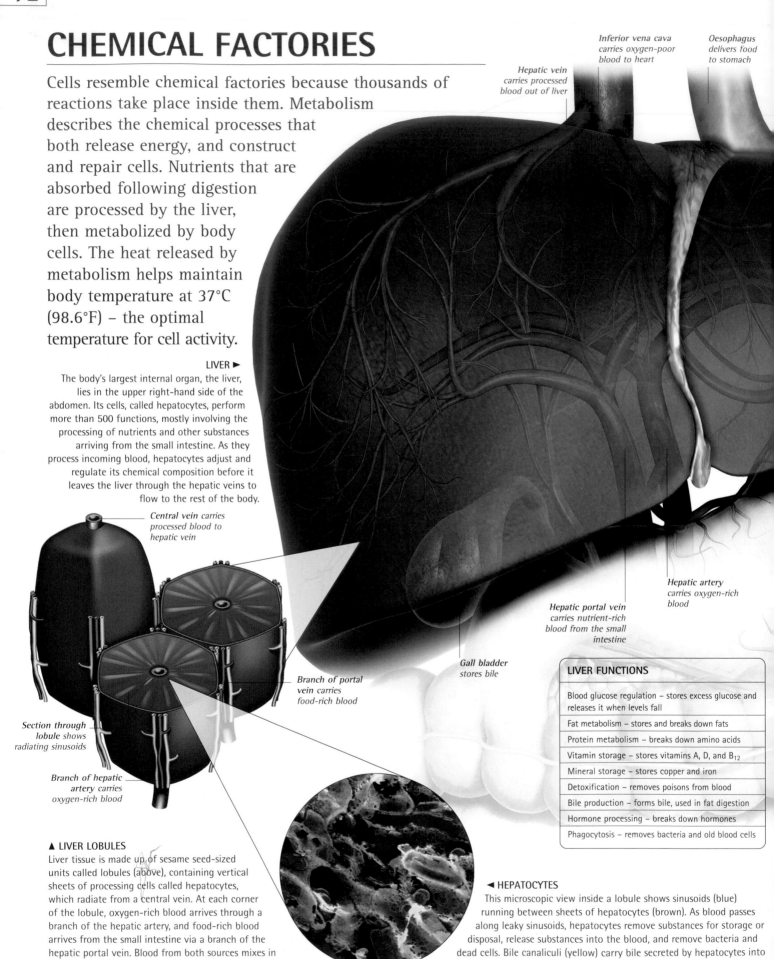

Inferior vena cava *carries oxygen-poor blood to heart*

Oesophagus *delivers food to stomach*

Hepatic vein *carries processed blood out of liver*

## LIVER ►
The body's largest internal organ, the liver, lies in the upper right-hand side of the abdomen. Its cells, called hepatocytes, perform more than 500 functions, mostly involving the processing of nutrients and other substances arriving from the small intestine. As they process incoming blood, hepatocytes adjust and regulate its chemical composition before it leaves the liver through the hepatic veins to flow to the rest of the body.

*Central vein carries processed blood to hepatic vein*

*Section through lobule shows radiating sinusoids*

*Branch of hepatic artery carries oxygen-rich blood*

*Branch of portal vein carries food-rich blood*

Hepatic artery *carries oxygen-rich blood*

Hepatic portal vein *carries nutrient-rich blood from the small intestine*

Gall bladder *stores bile*

### LIVER FUNCTIONS

| |
|---|
| Blood glucose regulation – stores excess glucose and releases it when levels fall |
| Fat metabolism – stores and breaks down fats |
| Protein metabolism – breaks down amino acids |
| Vitamin storage – stores vitamins A, D, and $B_{12}$ |
| Mineral storage – stores copper and iron |
| Detoxification – removes poisons from blood |
| Bile production – forms bile, used in fat digestion |
| Hormone processing – breaks down hormones |
| Phagocytosis – removes bacteria and old blood cells |

## ▲ LIVER LOBULES
Liver tissue is made up of sesame seed-sized units called lobules (above), containing vertical sheets of processing cells called hepatocytes, which radiate from a central vein. At each corner of the lobule, oxygen-rich blood arrives through a branch of the hepatic artery, and food-rich blood arrives from the small intestine via a branch of the hepatic portal vein. Blood from both sources mixes in spaces called sinusoids, which feed into the central vein.

## ◄ HEPATOCYTES
This microscopic view inside a lobule shows sinusoids (blue) running between sheets of hepatocytes (brown). As blood passes along leaky sinusoids, hepatocytes remove substances for storage or disposal, release substances into the blood, and remove bacteria and dead cells. Bile canaliculi (yellow) carry bile secreted by hepatocytes into bile ducts, which carry it to the duodenum where it is used in fat digestion.

## USING FOOD ►

To function normally, each body cell requires a supply of the simple nutrients extracted from food during digestion. During digestion, complex carbohydrates, fats, and proteins are digested in the small intestine into, respectively, glucose, fatty acids, and amino acids. These simple nutrients are absorbed through the small intestine and carried by the blood to the liver. Here they are processed or stored before being used by body cells.

*Food contains carbohydrates, fats, and proteins*

*Liver processes simple nutrients*

*Stomach begins process of digestion*

*Simple nutrients absorbed into bloodstream from small intestine*

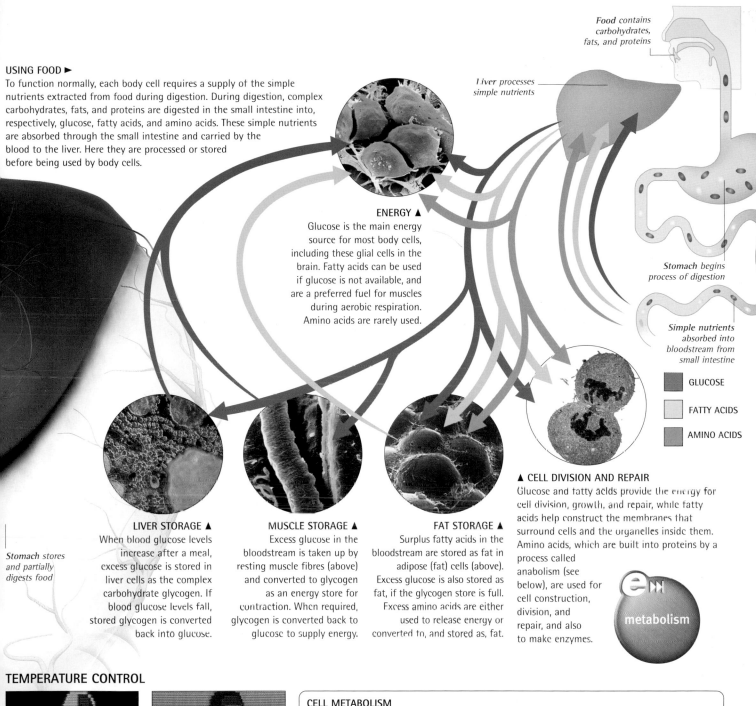

### ENERGY ▲
Glucose is the main energy source for most body cells, including these glial cells in the brain. Fatty acids can be used if glucose is not available, and are a preferred fuel for muscles during aerobic respiration. Amino acids are rarely used.

| | GLUCOSE |
| | FATTY ACIDS |
| | AMINO ACIDS |

*Stomach stores and partially digests food*

### LIVER STORAGE ▲
When blood glucose levels increase after a meal, excess glucose is stored in liver cells as the complex carbohydrate glycogen. If blood glucose levels fall, stored glycogen is converted back into glucose.

### MUSCLE STORAGE ▲
Excess glucose in the bloodstream is taken up by resting muscle fibres (above) and converted to glycogen as an energy store for contraction. When required, glycogen is converted back to glucose to supply energy.

### FAT STORAGE ▲
Surplus fatty acids in the bloodstream are stored as fat in adipose (fat) cells (above). Excess glucose is also stored as fat, if the glycogen store is full. Excess amino acids are either used to release energy or converted to, and stored as, fat.

### ▲ CELL DIVISION AND REPAIR
Glucose and fatty acids provide the energy for cell division, growth, and repair, while fatty acids help construct the membranes that surround cells and the organelles inside them. Amino acids, which are built into proteins by a process called anabolism (see below), are used for cell construction, division, and repair, and also to make enzymes.

**e ►► metabolism**

## TEMPERATURE CONTROL

### BEFORE SQUASH
Thermography is a type of imaging that shows how heat (generated by metabolism and by muscle contraction) is lost from the body. The colour code runs from white (hot) through yellow, red, blue, green, pale blue, purple to black (cool). Before squash, this player's thermogram is mostly pale blue and purple (medium to cool temperatures).

### AFTER SQUASH
After the game, extra heat generated during exercise is lost (under the control of the hypothalamus in the brain) to maintain a steady body temperature. Heat radiation through the player's skin increases, especially from his face. His surroundings also appear warmer because of the heat radiating from his body.

### CELL METABOLISM

Metabolism is the term used to describe the thousands of chemical reactions taking place continuously in body cells to keep the body alive and to generate energy. Cell metabolism has two closely linked parts – catabolism and anabolism. Both use nutrients absorbed during digestion and carried in the blood to cells.

Catabolic reactions break down energy-rich substances into simpler ones, releasing energy in the process. For example, during cell respiration, glucose is broken down into carbon dioxide and water. Anabolic reactions use the energy from catabolism to build simple molecules into complex ones. For example, amino acids are converted into proteins, which are used to build and run cells.

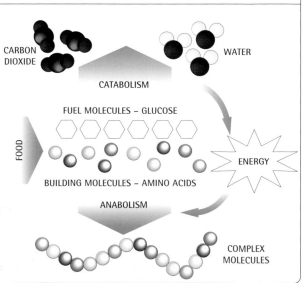

CARBON DIOXIDE

WATER

CATABOLISM

FUEL MOLECULES – GLUCOSE

FOOD

ENERGY

BUILDING MOLECULES – AMINO ACIDS

ANABOLISM

COMPLEX MOLECULES

# WASTE REMOVAL

Body cells continually deposit waste substances into the bloodstream that must be excreted, or removed, before they accumulate and poison the body. The kidneys, a pair of organs in the urinary system, play a major part in excretion by processing blood and removing wastes, such as urea. The kidneys also remove excess water from blood, so keeping its volume and composition constant. Wastes and excess water form urine, which is stored in the bladder and released several times a day. When the bladder is full, messages are relayed to the brain, warning a person of the need to urinate.

*Adrenal gland sits on top of kidney*

*Renal vein carries blood from kidney*

*Renal artery carries blood to kidney*

*Left kidney shown in section (detailed view opposite)*

*Right kidney is slightly lower than the left*

*Ureter carries urine to bladder from right kidney*

*Inferior vena cava carries oxygen-poor blood from lower body*

*Aorta carries oxygen-rich blood to lower body*

*Ureter carries urine to bladder from left kidney*

*Opening of right ureter into bladder*

*Urethra (female) carries urine from bladder to outside*

*Internal sphincter muscle controls release of urine*

*Bladder wall is muscular and elastic*

## ◄ URINARY SYSTEM

This body system consists of two kidneys, two ureters, the urinary bladder, and the urethra. The kidneys are packed with tiny filtering units called nephrons, which process blood to produce urine. The kidneys make up just one per cent of the body's mass, but they consume 25 per cent of its energy – an indication of their vital role. They process 1,750 litres (462 gallons) of blood daily to produce about 1.5 litres (2½ pt) of urine. Urine is squeezed down the ureters and stored in the bladder until is full. Then it is released through the urethra to the outside.

## ▲ LINING OF BLADDER WALL

The wall of the bladder consists largely of sheets of smooth muscle cells. When the bladder is empty, the muscles are fully contracted and the inner epithelial lining forms folds, called rugae, as shown in this SEM. As the bladder fills with up to 600 ml (1 pt) of urine, muscles in the wall relax and stretch, causing the folds to smooth out and disappear.

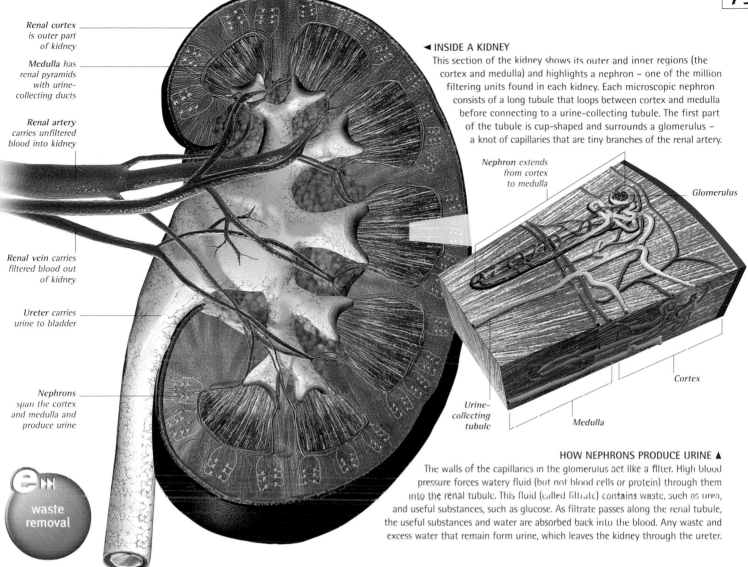

Renal cortex
is outer part
of kidney

Medulla has
renal pyramids
with urine-
collecting ducts

Renal artery
carries unfiltered
blood into kidney

Renal vein carries
filtered blood out
of kidney

Ureter carries
urine to bladder

Nephrons
span the cortex
and medulla and
produce urine

waste
removal

◀ INSIDE A KIDNEY

This section of the kidney shows its outer and inner regions (the cortex and medulla) and highlights a nephron – one of the million filtering units found in each kidney. Each microscopic nephron consists of a long tubule that loops between cortex and medulla before connecting to a urine-collecting tubule. The first part of the tubule is cup-shaped and surrounds a glomerulus – a knot of capillaries that are tiny branches of the renal artery.

Nephron extends
from cortex
to medulla

Glomerulus

Urine-
collecting
tubule

Medulla

Cortex

HOW NEPHRONS PRODUCE URINE ▲

The walls of the capillaries in the glomerulus act like a filter. High blood pressure forces watery fluid (but not blood cells or protein) through them into the renal tubule. This fluid (called filtrate) contains waste, such as urea, and useful substances, such as glucose. As filtrate passes along the renal tubule, the useful substances and water are absorbed back into the blood. Any waste and excess water that remain form urine, which leaves the kidney through the ureter.

## BLADDER FILLING AND EMPTYING

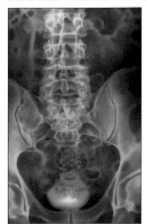

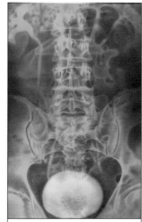

**EMPTY BLADDER**
This urogram shows a small bladder (green), which has been emptied recently. An internal sphincter – a muscular ring between the bladder and the urethra – holds urine inside. A lower external sphincter is formed by pelvic floor muscles around the urethra. The bladder fills as urine flows down the ureters from the kidneys.

**FULL BLADDER**
As the bladder fills, stretch receptors in its wall send messages to the spinal cord, which instructs the internal sphincter to relax. Messages also pass to the brain, and the person feels the need to urinate. When convenient, the person relaxes the external sphincter and the bladder contracts to push urine through the urethra.

### WATER BALANCE

To avoid becoming either bloated or dehydrated, the body matches the amount of water that enters it to the amount that leaves it. The figures below shows an adult's daily water intake and loss.

| SOURCE | WATER INTAKE |
|---|---|
| Metabolic water* | 250 ml (½ pt) |
| Food | 750 ml (1⅓ pt) |
| Drink | 1,500 ml (2⅔ pt) |
| Total | 2,500 ml (4½ pt) |

| SOURCE | WATER LOSS |
|---|---|
| Faeces | 100 ml (¼ pt) |
| Sweat | 200 ml (⅓ pt) |
| Lungs and skin** | 700 ml (1¼ pt) |
| Urine | 1,500 ml (2⅔ pt) |
| Total | 2,500 ml (4½ pt) |

* metabolic water = produced as a waste product of cell respiration
** includes water lost through the skin, but not as sweat

### TESTING URINE ▼

Urine tests identify abnormal levels of certain chemicals in urine (or chemicals not normally found there) to help doctors to diagnose disease. A dipstick with a pad that reacts to a specific chemical by changing colour is dipped into a urine sample and compared with a reference chart.

Colour chart used
to find match
with pad

Chemically treated
tip reacts to specific
chemical in urine

Wand held as
pad is dipped
in urine

# HUMAN REPRODUCTION

Organs in the male and female reproductive systems produce sex cells that enable adults to produce babies. This occurs when male and female sex cells meet after sexual intercourse. Inside the scrotum, a pair of oval glands called testes produce male sex cells (or sperm) continuously. Female sex cells (eggs or ova) are made by the ovaries and, during a woman's fertile years, are released one at a time in the middle of the menstrual cycle – a monthly sequence of changes that prepare the uterus for pregnancy.

reproduction

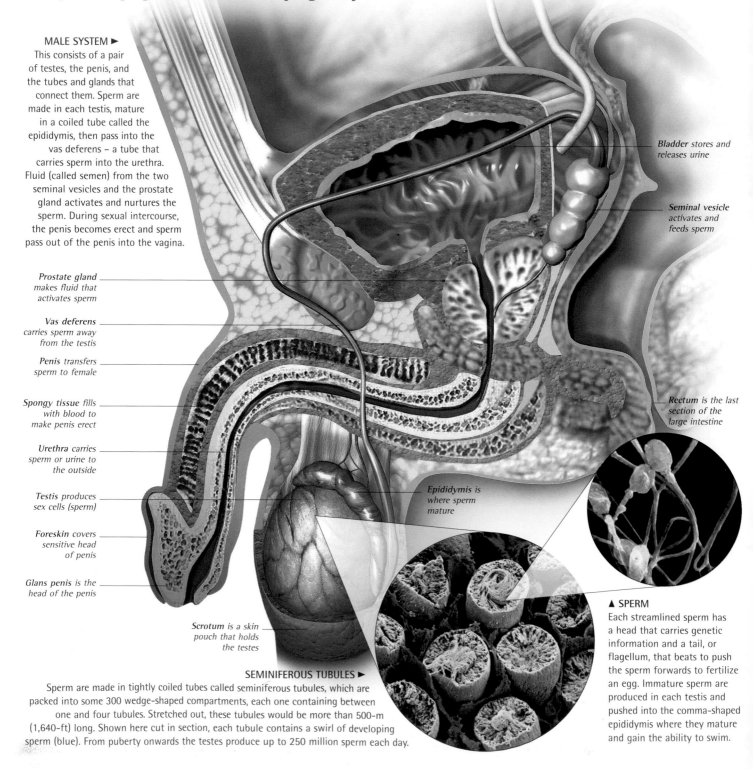

**MALE SYSTEM ▶**
This consists of a pair of testes, the penis, and the tubes and glands that connect them. Sperm are made in each testis, mature in a coiled tube called the epididymis, then pass into the vas deferens – a tube that carries sperm into the urethra. Fluid (called semen) from the two seminal vesicles and the prostate gland activates and nurtures the sperm. During sexual intercourse, the penis becomes erect and sperm pass out of the penis into the vagina.

*Prostate gland* makes fluid that activates sperm

*Vas deferens* carries sperm away from the testis

*Penis* transfers sperm to female

*Spongy tissue* fills with blood to make penis erect

*Urethra* carries sperm or urine to the outside

*Testis* produces sex cells (sperm)

*Foreskin* covers sensitive head of penis

*Glans penis* is the head of the penis

*Scrotum* is a skin pouch that holds the testes

*Bladder* stores and releases urine

*Seminal vesicle* activates and feeds sperm

*Rectum* is the last section of the large intestine

*Epididymis* is where sperm mature

**▲ SPERM**
Each streamlined sperm has a head that carries genetic information and a tail, or flagellum, that beats to push the sperm forwards to fertilize an egg. Immature sperm are produced in each testis and pushed into the comma-shaped epididymis where they mature and gain the ability to swim.

**SEMINIFEROUS TUBULES ▶**
Sperm are made in tightly coiled tubes called seminiferous tubules, which are packed into some 300 wedge-shaped compartments, each one containing between one and four tubules. Stretched out, these tubules would be more than 500-m (1,640-ft) long. Shown here cut in section, each tubule contains a swirl of developing sperm (blue). From puberty onwards the testes produce up to 250 million sperm each day.

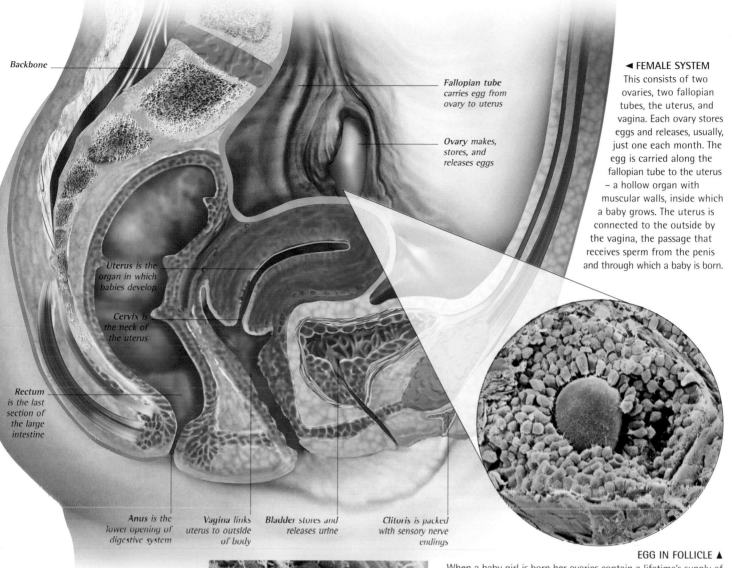

Backbone

Fallopian tube carries egg from ovary to uterus

Ovary makes, stores, and releases eggs

Uterus is the organ in which babies develop

Cervix is the neck of the uterus

Rectum is the last section of the large intestine

Anus is the lower opening of digestive system

Vagina links uterus to outside of body

Bladder stores and releases urine

Clitoris is packed with sensory nerve endings

## ◄ FEMALE SYSTEM

This consists of two ovaries, two fallopian tubes, the uterus, and vagina. Each ovary stores eggs and releases, usually, just one each month. The egg is carried along the fallopian tube to the uterus – a hollow organ with muscular walls, inside which a baby grows. The uterus is connected to the outside by the vagina, the passage that receives sperm from the penis and through which a baby is born.

## EGG IN FOLLICLE ▲

When a baby girl is born her ovaries contain a lifetime's supply of hundreds of thousands of immature eggs, each one inside a bag-like follicle. After puberty, a few follicles grow and mature each month. This SEM shows an egg (pink) inside a maturing follicle (green), surrounded by cells (blue) that nourish it. Each month, only one follicle matures fully – then bursts to release its egg.

## ▼ THE MENSTRUAL CYCLE AND OVULATION

During the menstrual cycle, which occurs every 28 days, the lining of the uterus thickens ready to receive an embryo. Around day 14 of the cycle, ovulation occurs – an egg is released from a mature follicle. If the egg is fertilized, the resulting embryo implants in the uterus. If the egg is not fertilized, the lining of the uterus breaks down and is shed during menstruation (a period).

## ◄ LINING OF THE UTERUS

This SEM shows the surface of the lining of the uterus (endometrium) midway through the menstrual cycle. Food-rich globules (yellow) are being secreted by glands ready to nurture an embryo, should one implant in the lining. If an egg is fertilized, the embryo that results will burrow into the blood-rich endometrium to continue its development into a baby.

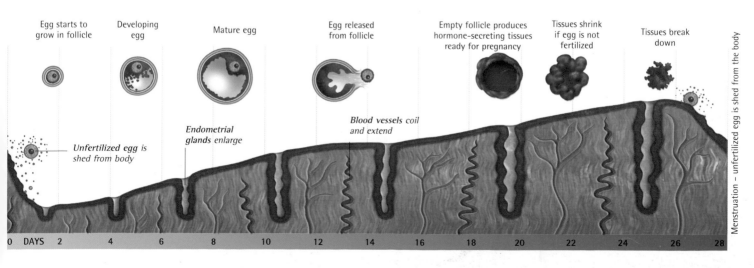

Egg starts to grow in follicle

Developing egg

Mature egg

Egg released from follicle

Empty follicle produces hormone-secreting tissues ready for pregnancy

Tissues shrink if egg is not fertilized

Tissues break down

Unfertilized egg is shed from body

Endometrial glands enlarge

Blood vessels coil and extend

Menstruation – unfertilized egg is shed from the body

0   DAYS   2        4        6        8        10        12        14        16        18        20        22        24        26        28

# PREGNANCY AND BIRTH

If a male sperm and a female egg meet, fertilization occurs. The fertilized egg, or zygote, implants in the uterus wall, where it continues its growth and development as an embryo. After eight weeks, it becomes a fetus and over the remaining weeks and months is transformed into a fully developed baby. During labour and birth, which occurs after about 40 weeks of pregnancy, the baby is pushed out of the uterus and into the outside world.

**OVULATION ►**

This SEM shows an egg emerging from an ovary after being released from the follicle that lies just below the surface. This process of ovulation occurs once a month in women between puberty and the menopause (at around age 50). The egg passes into a fallopian tube and is wafted towards the uterus by hair-like cilia.

*Ovum (female egg) bursts from its follicle*

**SPERM IN UTERUS ►**

Between two and three hundred million sperm are deposited in the vagina following sexual intercourse. Only a small proportion of sperm make it through the cervix to the uterus, like those shown here. They take 12 to 24 hours to reach the fallopian tube in search of an egg.

*Sperm swimming through uterus*

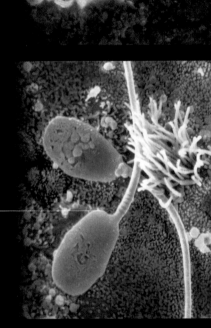

**◄ FERTILIZATION**

If sperm meet an egg within 24 hours of ovulation, fertilization may occur. Sperm surround the egg and try to penetrate its outer layer. One sperm eventually succeeds. It enters the egg and loses its tail. Its head, which contains genetic material, fuses with the nucleus of the egg. The egg is now fertilized.

*Ovum has a thick, outer layer*

**FOUR-CELL ZYGOTE ►**

About 36 hours after the egg has been fertilized, it divides into two. After 48 hours, it has divided again to form a zygote like this one, which consists of four cells. The zygote is travelling along the fallopian tube towards the uterus. As it does so, its cells continue to divide every 12 hours.

*Zygote consists of four cells*

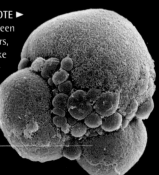

**◄ IMPLANTATION**

Now called a blastocyst, this six-day-old hollow cluster of cells is attaching itself to the uterus wall by burrowing into the lining. This process is called implantation. The blastocyst's inner cells form the embryo, which will develop into a baby, while the outer cells help form the placenta.

*Blastocyst implants in the lining of the uterus*

# FETAL GROWTH AND DEVELOPMENT

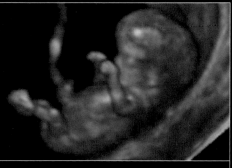

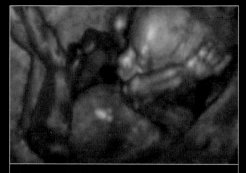

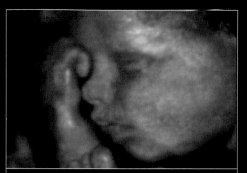

### FETUS AT 10 WEEKS
Ultrasound is a safe technique used to monitor fetal growth and development. This sequence of 3-D images have been produced using the latest ultrasound techniques. At ten weeks the 5 cm (2 in) fetus is recognizably human, although the head is large in proportion to the body. All internal organs are in place and the limbs are formed.

### FETUS AT 16 WEEKS
At 16 weeks, the fetus is about 15 cm (6 in) long, and is growing rapidly as its body systems develop, and moving vigorously. Arms, legs, fingers, and toes can be seen clearly, as can facial features. The fetal heartbeat can be detected, as can the sex of the fetus. Facial muscles allow the fetus to open and close its mouth.

### FETUS AT 30 WEEKS
By 30 weeks, the fetus is about 35 cm (14 in) in length and is reaching full development. During the final weeks of pregnancy, a layer of fat develops under the skin. The ears can detect sounds from inside or outside the mother's body. The mother can feel the movements of the fetus as it kicks and turns inside the uterus. ·

*Uterus surrounds and protects fetus*

*Umbilical cord carries blood to fetus*

*Placenta is attached to inside of uterus*

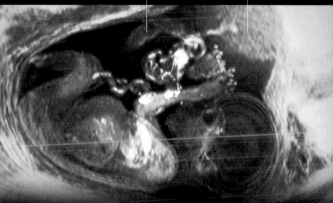

**pregnancy and birth**

## ▲ PLACENTA AND UMBILICAL CORD
This MRI scan of a fetus shows the placenta and umbilical cord, which together supply all its needs. Fetal and maternal blood vessels are not connected but come into close contact inside the placenta, a disc of tissue on the inner surface of the uterus. Oxygen and food pass from the mother's blood into that of the fetus, while wastes pass in the opposite direction. The umbilical cord carries blood between the fetus and placenta.

## THE PREGNANT BODY

A number of changes occur to a woman's body during pregnancy as it adjusts to the needs of her growing fetus.

Both her breathing and heart rate increase as she delivers oxygen and food to the fetus via the placenta, and removes its wastes.

Her weight increases as her uterus and abdomen expand to house the growing fetus. Her breasts swell as new milk glands develop ready to supply the baby with milk after it is born.

*Developing fetus inside woman's body*

### BIRTH ►
A baby is born when it is fully developed, usually around 38 to 40 weeks after fertilization. When the mother goes into labour, the muscular walls of her uterus contract to push the baby out. Once delivered, the baby responds to the sudden change in surroundings and starts breathing. The umbilical cord is clamped and cut.

# GROWING CHILD

In the first five years, a child's brain grows rapidly in size and complexity, allowing the child to practise and master increasingly difficult skills. Many of these are essential for survival. As bones and muscles grow, the child progresses from crawling to walking and develops manual dexterity through handling toys and other objects. From age one onwards, children use language to communicate and gradually develop social skills, such as eating with a knife and fork.

### ◄ NEWBORN
A newborn baby sleeps for up to 18 hours a day punctuated by regular liquid feeds. He is startled by loud noise and shows certain reflex actions, such as the sucking reflex, which help to ensure his survival. He watches his mother's face intently and at four to six weeks old, begins to smile.

*Newborn sleeps curled up as in uterus*

growing child

### CRAWLING ►
At eight to nine months old, a baby can usually crawl on all fours and tries to stand holding on to a support. He can grasp objects between thumb and finger, prod small objects with his index finger, hold a cup, and grasp and chew solid food. He shouts to attract attention.

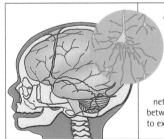

*Arms support infant when crawling*

## MILESTONES

As they grow, children pass specific milestones of development in a predictable order. This order is determined by the increasing maturity of the child's nervous system. The speed at which the nervous system matures dictates how rapidly children learn particular skills. This is why individual children progress at their own rate.

| SKILL | FIRST DEVELOPS |
|---|---|
| First smile | 4–6 weeks |
| First word | 12–14 months |
| Potty trained | 18–30 months |
| Social play | 3–4 years |
| Complex speech | 4–5 years |
| Reading | 5–6 years |
| Complex reasoning | 10–12 years |

## BRAIN AND SKULL

### AT BIRTH
The brain's 100 billion neurons (nerve cells) are already present at birth and start to contact each other to form a neural communication network (in circle, left). At birth, this network is poorly developed. Gaps between skull bones allow the skull to expand and grow with the brain.

### AT 6 YEARS
The brain grows rapidly and approaches full size at the age of six. This growth results from the enormous increase in the number of connections in the neural network as the child learns. The gaps between skull bones are now closed, and the skull grows at a slower rate.

*Balance improves with practice*

## BABY TEETH

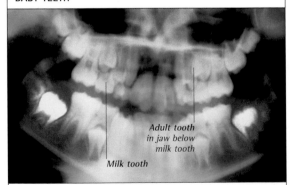

*Adult tooth in jaw below milk tooth*

*Milk tooth*

We have two sets of teeth during our lifetime. Milk, or deciduous, teeth first appear at six months, and all 20 are in place by the age of three. Permanent teeth develop in the jaw underneath and start appearing around the age of six, dislodging the milk teeth, which then fall out. The adult's full set of 32 teeth is in place by the end of the teens. This X-ray of a child's mouth shows adult teeth below the milk teeth. Adult molar teeth in the lower jaw appear light yellow.

### AT 18 YEARS
During the teen years, the neural network develops more slowly than earlier. By the age of 18, the brain is at full size and the neural network fully developed, although it will be modified continually throughout life. The skull is fully sized and the face shows its adult features.

### ▲ WALKING
At 12 to 14 months old, a child can walk if her hand is held and can negotiate obstacles by stepping sideways. She speaks her first words and understand simple commands. She holds o her arms and feet to be dresse and can grasp objects delicate then drop them.

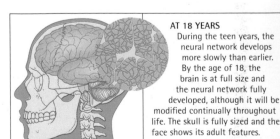

## HOW BONES DEVELOP

### NEWBORN BABY'S BONE
In a newborn baby, the shafts of long bones, such as finger bones, are made of bone tissue, and the bone ends are cartilage. Between the shaft and each bone end is another zone of cartilage called a growth plate, in which cells divide to produce more cartilage and make the bone grow longer.

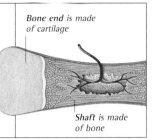

*Bone end is made of cartilage*

*Shaft is made of bone*

### CHILD'S BONE
Babies and children have bone-making regions in the ends of bones. These gradually replace cartilage with hard, bony tissue. In the growth plates located between the shaft and bone end, cells divide to form more cartilage to push the bone ends outwards. This causes the bone to grow in length.

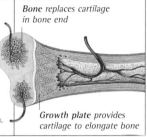

*Bone replaces cartilage in bone end*

*Growth plate provides cartilage to elongate bone*

### ADULT BONE
By the age of 18 when the body has nearly finished growing, the shaft, ends, and growth plates of long bones have ossified and fused into a single bone. Other types of bones, such as short bones, are also ossified by now. However, bones continue to reshape throughout adult life.

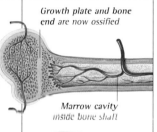

*Growth plate and bone end are now ossified*

*Marrow cavity inside bone shaft*

## HAND GROWTH

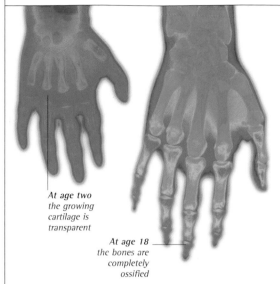

*At age two the growing cartilage is transparent*

*At age 18 the bones are completely ossified*

These X-rays show the changes that occur to the bones of the hand between the ages of two (top left) and 18 (top right). In the young fetus, the skeleton consists of cartilage "bones". As the fetus grows, the shafts (central sections) of these bones are replaced by bone through a process called ossification ("bone making").

The X-ray showing the hand of a two year old reveals the outline of his partly ossified bones. The more defined areas show the bony shafts, and the see-through (transparent) parts show where the cartilage is still growing. These areas will eventually be replaced by hard bone.

The results of this process can be clearly seen in the X-ray of the hand of an 18 year old. Here, bones are fully grown in length and fully ossified. X rays are a reliable indication of the age of a growing child because bones ossify at predictable ages.

### ◀ PEDALLING
Between the ages of two and three, a child gains new skills as his co-ordination improves. He can run around, ride a tricycle, kick a ball, open doors, and put on his shoes. He speaks in simple sentences and asks for things. As he plays, he learns to share with other children.

*Improved co-ordination allows child to pedal and steer*

*Hand eye co-ordination enables child to catch ball*

### THROWING AND CATCHING BALLS ▶
By the age of five, hand eye co-ordination has improved sufficiently for a child to catch a ball. She can run lightly on her toes, stand on tiptoe, and dance in time to music. Her speech is grammatical and understandable, she can write and read, draw objects, copy shapes, and dress and undress.

# LIFE STORY

Throughout life every human being follows the same, predictable sequence of changes – infancy, childhood, adolescence, adulthood, and old age. As children grow, they learn and develop life skills. During adolescence they undergo rapid physical changes, called puberty, as well as a change in behaviour and attitudes. Adulthood brings new challenges and responsibility and, for many men and women, children of their own. As people age, the body starts to become less efficient.

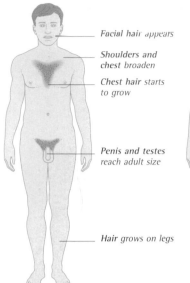

▲ PUBERTY – BOYS

Facial hair appears

Shoulders and chest broaden

Chest hair starts to grow

Penis and testes reach adult size

Hair grows on legs

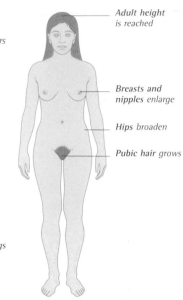

▲ PUBERTY – GIRLS

Adult height is reached

Breasts and nipples enlarge

Hips broaden

Pubic hair grows

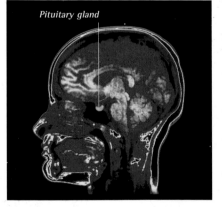

◄ CHILDHOOD
Childhood generally begins when a child is able to walk and talk and ends at puberty. During the intervening years, children acquire skills rapidly, increasing their store of knowledge as they learn to read and write. They develop social skills, and once they are able to understand another person's point of view, become better at self-discipline, playing games, and making friends. All children gain physical and mental skills in the same order but have their own strengths and weaknesses.

▲ PUBERTY – BOYS
Male puberty usually begins between the ages of 12 and 14. First, the testes enlarge, release testosterone, and start to produce sperm. The penis begins to grow, reaching its adult size after about two years. The body grows rapidly into its muscular adult shape with broader shoulders. Hair begins to grow in the armpits and in the pubic region and, later on, on the face and chest. As a boy's larynx enlarges, his voice becomes deeper. Teenage boys continue to grow for several years after puberty, which is why men are usually taller than women.

▲ PUBERTY – GIRLS
Female puberty usually begins between the ages of 10 and 12, with the first menstrual period occurring about two years later. Initially, the breasts and nipples start to enlarge as do the ovaries. After a period of rapid growth, the distribution of body fat around the body changes and girls assume a more womanly shape with broader hips. Pubic and armpit hair grows, and menstrual periods begin, followed by the release of the first eggs. Teenage girls are usually taller than boys of the same age but stop growing sooner.

## CHANGES AT PUBERTY

Pituitary gland

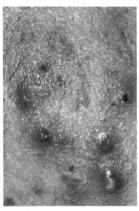

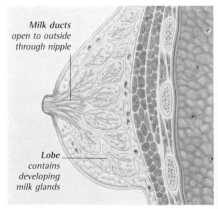

Milk ducts open to outside through nipple

Lobe contains developing milk glands

▲ PITUITARY GLAND
Puberty is triggered by the hypothalamus in the brain (see p.44), which signals to the pituitary gland (above) to release two hormones, FSH and LH. In girls, FSH and LH instruct the ovaries to release eggs, and to secrete the female sex hormones oestrogen and progesterone, which produce female sexual characteristics. In boys, FSH and LH boosts the secretion of the hormone testosterone by the testes – producing male sexual characteristics and stimulating sperm production.

▲ ACNE
Many teenagers are troubled by acne – a persistent rash of sore, red spots on the face and back. Hormonal changes in girls and boys increase the secretion of oily sebum by the sebaceous glands in the skin. Spots form if ducts from these glands get blocked and the sebum is infected by bacteria.

▲ BEARD GROWTH
Increasing levels of the male sex hormone testosterone in males stimulates the growth of thicker terminal hairs (like scalp hairs) on the face, chest, and legs. Facial hair can be removed by shaving. This SEM shows beard hairs that have been shaved and are now growing back.

▲ BREAST DEVELOPMENT
The growth of the breasts is often one of the first signs of puberty in girls. The breast grows as the mammary gland develops inside it. As this section through a breast shows, the mammary gland consists of lobes that radiate out from the nipple. Inside the lobes are milk glands that will produce milk following the birth of a baby. The milk glands release their milk along ducts and through the nipple, which also enlarges during puberty.

## LIFE FACTS

| | |
|---|---|
| Peak age for learning | Childhood and teens |
| Peak age for physical fitness | Mid-twenties to thirties |
| Peak age for fertility | Mid-twenties to early thirties |
| Intellectual peak and plateau | Mid-thirties to late fifties |
| Life expectancy at birth in Western world (male) | 74 years |
| Life expectancy at birth in Western world (female) | 80 years |

*Skin becomes less elastic and wrinkles*

adulthood

*Glasses become essential for most people as they get older*

### ▲ PRIME OF LIFE

The 20s and 30s are the time in the life cycle when humans are at their peak. Men and women are at their fittest and healthiest, have the most opportunities, develop their careers, travel, make friends, form relationships, and start families. However, by the end of her 20s, a woman's fertility is already starting to decline, and the older she gets, the more difficult it may be to conceive. A good diet, sensible lifestyle, and regular exercise increase the chance of good health later in life.

### OLD AGE ►

From their late 50s onwards, people begin to age visibly. Wrinkles appear as the skin loses its elasticity. Sight and hearing become less efficient; hair thins and turns grey; muscles lose strength; bones may become brittle and joints may become less mobile. Some effects of ageing can be minimized by a healthy lifestyle. People in Western countries are living longer than ever, thanks to improved living conditions and healthcare.

## PROBLEMS OF AGEING

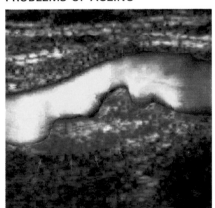

### ▲ NARROWED ARTERY

As some people get older, their arteries become narrowed by a build-up of fatty deposits on artery walls. These can be caused by factors such as a high-fat diet or smoking. A build-up (marked with pink arrows above) creates activity in the blood flow (orange) around it, as picked up by this Doppler ultrasound scan of an artery. Where this turbulence occurs, a blood clot may form. If the clot blocks an artery that supplies the heart muscle, it can cause a heart attack.

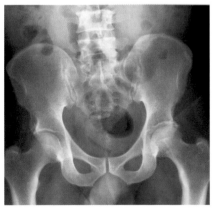

### ▲ OSTEOARTHRITIS

This X-ray of a man's pelvis shows areas of osteoarthritis (orange), a degenerative change that often affects weight-bearing joints, such as the knees or hips, as people get older. It is caused by the wearing away of the friction-reducing cartilage that covers bone ends in joints. As a result the joints get stiff and painful. The two femurs (upper leg bones) are usually separated from their sockets in the pelvis by cartilage, but here the joint spaces have narrowed.

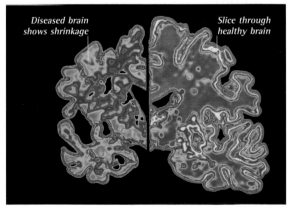

*Diseased brain shows shrinkage*

*Slice through healthy brain*

### ▲ ALZHEIMER'S DISEASE

Although the brain begins to deteriorate in later life, the effects of this are usually unnoticeable – most people find ways to compensate for small memory lapses. However, a disease such as Alzheimer's causes severe problems. This progressive decrease in mental ability affects 7 people in every 100 by the age of 65, and 30 in 100 by the age of 85. The two brain scans (above) show how the brain of a person with Alzheimer's disease has shrunk because of the loss of brain cells and deposits of abnormal proteins. This degeneration causes confusion, memory loss, and personality changes – and often loss of independence, too.

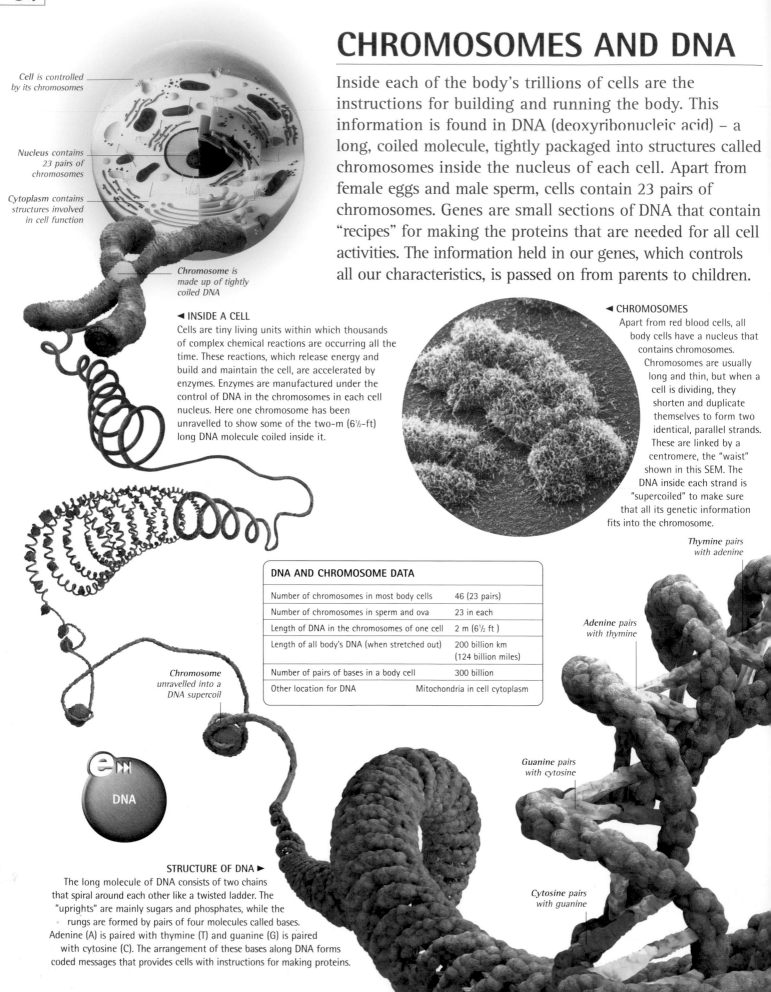

Cell is controlled
by its chromosomes

Nucleus contains
23 pairs of
chromosomes

Cytoplasm contains
structures involved
in cell function

Chromosome is
made up of tightly
coiled DNA

# CHROMOSOMES AND DNA

Inside each of the body's trillions of cells are the instructions for building and running the body. This information is found in DNA (deoxyribonucleic acid) – a long, coiled molecule, tightly packaged into structures called chromosomes inside the nucleus of each cell. Apart from female eggs and male sperm, cells contain 23 pairs of chromosomes. Genes are small sections of DNA that contain "recipes" for making the proteins that are needed for all cell activities. The information held in our genes, which controls all our characteristics, is passed on from parents to children.

◄ INSIDE A CELL

Cells are tiny living units within which thousands of complex chemical reactions are occurring all the time. These reactions, which release energy and build and maintain the cell, are accelerated by enzymes. Enzymes are manufactured under the control of DNA in the chromosomes in each cell nucleus. Here one chromosome has been unravelled to show some of the two-m (6½-ft) long DNA molecule coiled inside it.

◄ CHROMOSOMES

Apart from red blood cells, all body cells have a nucleus that contains chromosomes. Chromosomes are usually long and thin, but when a cell is dividing, they shorten and duplicate themselves to form two identical, parallel strands. These are linked by a centromere, the "waist" shown in this SEM. The DNA inside each strand is "supercoiled" to make sure that all its genetic information fits into the chromosome.

Chromosome
unravelled into a
DNA supercoil

DNA

### DNA AND CHROMOSOME DATA

| | |
|---|---|
| Number of chromosomes in most body cells | 46 (23 pairs) |
| Number of chromosomes in sperm and ova | 23 in each |
| Length of DNA in the chromosomes of one cell | 2 m (6½ ft ) |
| Length of all body's DNA (when stretched out) | 200 billion km (124 billion miles) |
| Number of pairs of bases in a body cell | 300 billion |
| Other location for DNA | Mitochondria in cell cytoplasm |

Thymine pairs
with adenine

Adenine pairs
with thymine

Guanine pairs
with cytosine

Cytosine pairs
with guanine

STRUCTURE OF DNA ►

The long molecule of DNA consists of two chains that spiral around each other like a twisted ladder. The "uprights" are mainly sugars and phosphates, while the rungs are formed by pairs of four molecules called bases. Adenine (A) is paired with thymine (T) and guanine (G) is paired with cytosine (C). The arrangement of these bases along DNA forms coded messages that provides cells with instructions for making proteins.

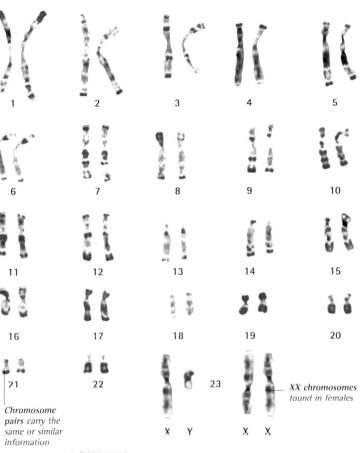

1 2 3 4 5
6 7 8 9 10
11 12 13 14 15
16 17 18 19 20
21 22 23

*XX chromosomes found in females*

X Y X X

*Chromosome pairs carry the same or similar information*

## ▲ KARYOTYPE

A karyotype like the one above shows a complete set of 23 pairs of human chromosomes. The chromosomes are photographed when they become short and thick during cell division and arranged as pairs 1 to 22 in order of size. One member of each pair comes from a person's mother and one from the father. The 23rd pair is the sex chromosomes – either XY in males or XX in females. Both are shown here.

## DOWN'S SYNDROME

Named after the 19th-century doctor who first described it, Down's syndrome is an abnormality in the number of chromosomes that results in children being born with a variety of disabilities. Down's children usually have slightly slanted eyes, stubby fingers, a large tongue, flattened facial features, and some learning difficulties. However, they are friendly and affectionate children and most are able to lead fulfilling lives.

The condition is also called trisomy 21 because an extra chromosome 21 is passed on by one parent, usually the mother, making a total of 47 chromosomes. It is this extra chromosome that causes the problem. The risk of having a baby with Down's syndrome increases with the age of the mother.

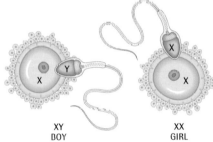

XY BOY    XX GIRL

## ◀ SEX DETERMINATION

Sex cells – sperm and eggs – each contain one set of 23 chromosomes. When a sperm fertilizes an egg, the two sets join to make a complement of 46. One chromosome in each of the sets is a sex chromosome. This is always an X chromosome in an egg, but either an X or a Y chromosome in a sperm. The sperm dictates whether a fertilized egg develops into a boy or girl. An egg fertilized by a Y-carrying sperm produces a boy. An egg fertilized by an X-carrying sperm produces a girl.

## MAKING PROTEINS

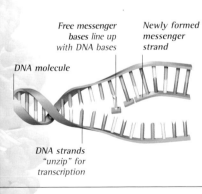

*Free messenger bases line up with DNA bases*  *Newly formed messenger strand*  *DNA molecule*  *DNA strands "unzip" for transcription*

### TRANSCRIPTION

A major function of DNA is to provide instructions for making the proteins that make up structures such as skin, or hormones, or enzymes. A sequence of bases in a small section of DNA (a gene) acts as a template. The section "unzips" and its pattern of bases is matched by free messenger bases (called mRNA bases), which line up beneath one strand. These link up to form a messsenger strand that moves into the cell cytoplasm and instructs the building of a protein.

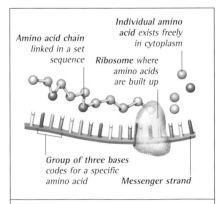

*Amino acid chain linked in a set sequence*  *Individual amino acid exists freely in cytoplasm*  *Ribosome where amino acids are built up*  *Group of three bases codes for a specific amino acid*  *Messenger strand*

### TRANSLATION

In the cytoplasm, a particle called a ribosome provides the site where the new messenger strand will be turned into a protein, according to the genetic code. Each group of three bases on the messenger strand carries instructions for a specific amino acid. As the messenger passes through the ribosome, amino acids, which exist freely in the cytoplasm, line up in the "correct" order and then link together to form a protein chain.

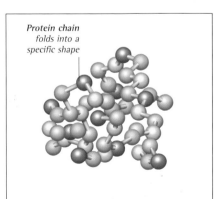

*Protein chain folds into a specific shape*

### COMPLETED PROTEIN

When the completed protein has been manufactured, it folds up to form the newly completed protein. Its specific shape is determined by the exact order of the amino acids that are used to build it and is the key to the way the protein will function. By controlling the manufacture of these key chemicals, DNA controls the purpose and function of all body cells and hence the growth and development of all body organs and tissues.

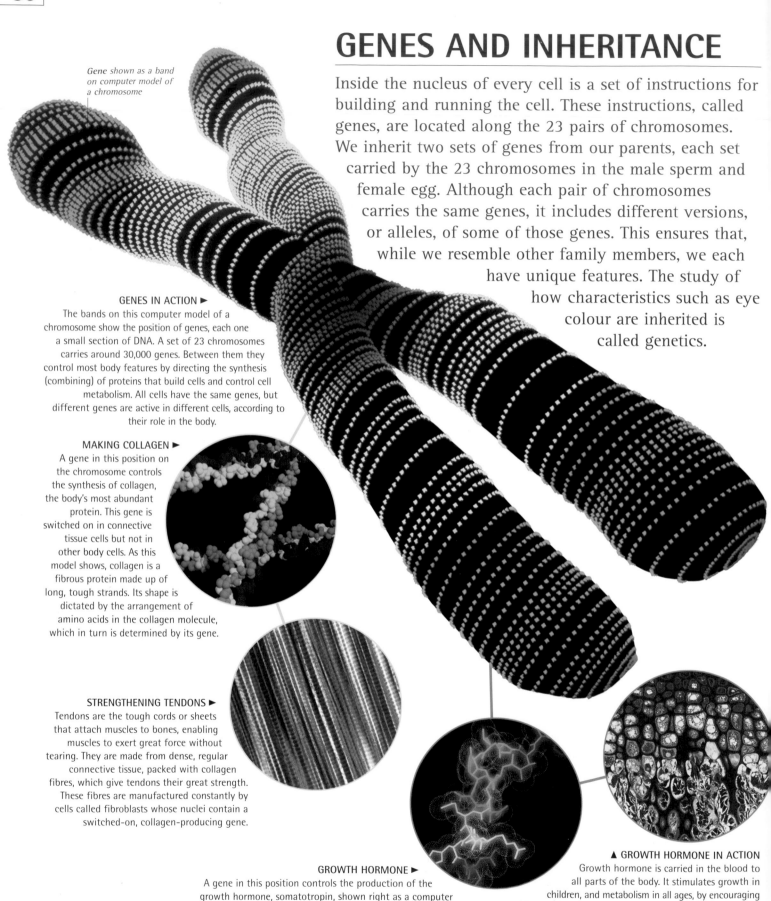

*Gene shown as a band on computer model of a chromosome*

# GENES AND INHERITANCE

Inside the nucleus of every cell is a set of instructions for building and running the cell. These instructions, called genes, are located along the 23 pairs of chromosomes. We inherit two sets of genes from our parents, each set carried by the 23 chromosomes in the male sperm and female egg. Although each pair of chromosomes carries the same genes, it includes different versions, or alleles, of some of those genes. This ensures that, while we resemble other family members, we each have unique features. The study of how characteristics such as eye colour are inherited is called genetics.

**GENES IN ACTION ▶**
The bands on this computer model of a chromosome show the position of genes, each one a small section of DNA. A set of 23 chromosomes carries around 30,000 genes. Between them they control most body features by directing the synthesis (combining) of proteins that build cells and control cell metabolism. All cells have the same genes, but different genes are active in different cells, according to their role in the body.

**MAKING COLLAGEN ▶**
A gene in this position on the chromosome controls the synthesis of collagen, the body's most abundant protein. This gene is switched on in connective tissue cells but not in other body cells. As this model shows, collagen is a fibrous protein made up of long, tough strands. Its shape is dictated by the arrangement of amino acids in the collagen molecule, which in turn is determined by its gene.

**STRENGTHENING TENDONS ▶**
Tendons are the tough cords or sheets that attach muscles to bones, enabling muscles to exert great force without tearing. They are made from dense, regular connective tissue, packed with collagen fibres, which give tendons their great strength. These fibres are manufactured constantly by cells called fibroblasts whose nuclei contain a switched-on, collagen-producing gene.

**GROWTH HORMONE ▶**
A gene in this position controls the production of the growth hormone, somatotropin, shown right as a computer model. This hormone is made by cells in the anterior (front) part of the pituitary gland – a pea-sized hormone-producing gland sitting just below the brain. The gene that controls the synthesis of growth hormone is switched on inside pituitary gland cells but is switched off inside other body cells.

**▲ GROWTH HORMONE IN ACTION**
Growth hormone is carried in the blood to all parts of the body. It stimulates growth in children, and metabolism in all ages, by encouraging cell growth and division, and the burning of fats for fuel. In children, the hormone's major targets are bone and muscle. This section through a growing bone shows ossification – columns of cartilage being replaced by bone. This process is stimulated directly by growth hormone.

## ▲ GENES AND GENERATIONS

This photograph shows four generations from the same family – great-grandmother, grandmother, mother, and daughter. The family resemblance is clear, but each member has distinct characteristics because, although most of their genes are identical, a few are not. Each person is the product of the combination of genes that results when a sperm fertilizes an egg. This produces a unique mix of genes, ensuring that a daughter is not identical to either her mother or father.

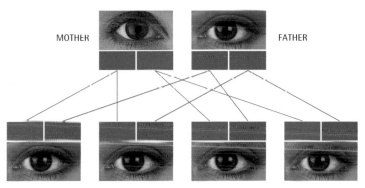

MOTHER     FATHER

CHILDREN

## ▲ GENES AND ALLELES

Genes occur in different versions called alleles, and it is these differences that produce the variations between us. The gene that controls eye colour, for example, can produce blue eyes or brown eyes. If both blue and brown alleles are inherited, only the brown allele has any effect. It is said to be dominant because it does not "allow" expression of the blue allele, which is called recessive. The diagrams above and below show how inheritance of eye colour works.

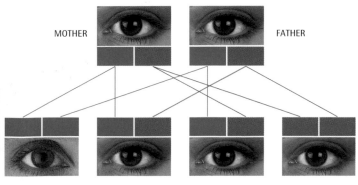

MOTHER     FATHER

CHILDREN

## ▲ THE GENETICS OF EYE COLOUR

Where the mother is blue eyed (having two blue alleles) and the father is brown-eyed (having two brown alleles) their children will inherit both blue and brown alleles but will have brown eyes. This is because the brown allele is dominant. If both parents are brown eyed, but each have both brown and blue alleles, there is a one in four chance that their child will inherit two blue alleles and have blue eyes, and a three in four chance that a child will be brown eyed.

ALLELE FOR BLUE EYES       ALLELE FOR BROWN EYES

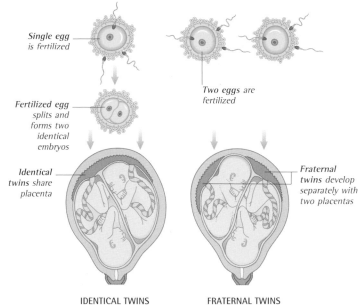

*Single egg* is fertilized

*Two eggs* are fertilized

*Fertilized egg* splits and forms two identical embryos

*Identical twins* share placenta

*Fraternal twins* develop separately with two placentas

IDENTICAL TWINS      FRATERNAL TWINS

## ▲ TWINS

Around one in 66 births produces twins. Identical twins are produced when a single fertilized egg splits into two separate cells that share identical genes. Fraternal twins result from two eggs being released at the same time, and each being fertilized by a different sperm. The resulting twins, although the same age, are no more alike than any other sisters or brothers, and may be the same or different sexes.

## GENES AND ENVIRONMENT ▶

Although it may seem impossible to distinguish between these genetically identical twins, each of these young women may differ strongly in personality or personal taste. It is not just the genes we inherit that determine the way we look and behave – our environment and experiences also influence what we are. Each twin is an individual because of what happens to her during her life.

## GENETIC DISORDER

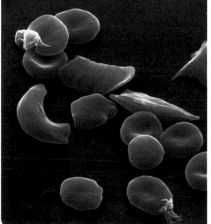

A genetic disorder is caused when a faulty gene or genes are inherited from one or both parents. Sickle cell disease, for example, is caused by a defect in the gene that controls production of oxygen-carrying haemoglobin inside red blood cells. This fault causes abnormalities in the shape of red blood cells.

A person with sickle cell anaemia inherits two copies of the faulty gene – one from each parent. As blood passes through oxygen-poor tissues, red blood cells curve into a sickle shape (left), blocking blood vessels and causing pain. Sickle cell trait – a much milder disease, often without symptoms– occurs when a person inherits one normal and one faulty copy of the gene.

# HUMAN GENOME

The human genome is all the DNA in one set of 23 chromosomes and contains the genes (instructions) for making a human being. Scientists working for the Human Genome Project have looked at the way the four bases – adenine (A), cytosine (C), guanine (G), and thymine (T) – are arranged in pairs along the DNA of individuals. Of the 3.2 billion pairs, only 0.1 per cent differ between the genomes of any two people. These differences make us individuals. Researchers are also finding out which fragments represent genes. There are about 30,000 genes in total, separated by stretches of "junk" DNA that have no function.

**HUMAN GENOME PROJECT (HGP) ►**
Started in 1990, the HGP is an international research project with two aims. The first aim – to find out the precise order of the bases A, C, G, and T in the DNA of the human genome – was achieved by April 2003. The second aim is to make a complete map of the genome showing which genes are found in which location. This part of the project is continuing.

**▲ READING DNA**
Each DNA molecule consists of a ladder-like chain of the bases adenine, cytosine, guanine, and thymine (see p.84). Scientists have found ways of reading the order, or sequence, of bases along a DNA molecule just as you are reading letters in order in this sentence. The first step is to cut the long DNA molecule into shorter strands of varying length. Then the strands are colour coded (above) and "read" by a computer that works out the order of bases in each strand. It puts the strands back together - like the pieces of a jigsaw - to reveal the sequence of the entire DNA molecule.

Technician uses a multi-channel pipette to put DNA into wells

Wells in tray contain DNA for sequencing

| GENOME FACTS | |
|---|---|
| Number of genes in human genome | 30,000 |
| Number of DNA bases ("letters") in the genome | 3.2 billion |
| Pile of books filled by "letters" in a genome | 60-m (197-ft) high |
| Amount of DNA in genome in genes | 3 % |
| Amount of "junk" DNA not in genes | 97 % |
| Similarity of DNA in genome of identical twins | 100 % |
| Similarity of DNA in genome of two siblings | 99.95 % |
| Similarity of DNA in genome of two unrelated humans | 99.9 % |
| Similarity of DNA in genome of human and chimp | 98 % |

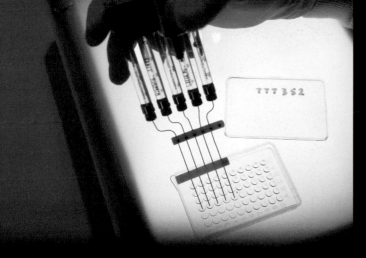

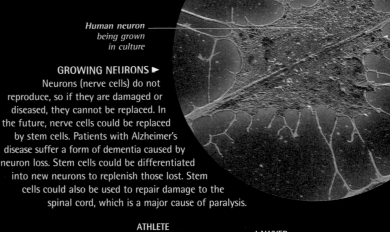

Human neuron being grown in culture

### GROWING NEURONS ▶
Neurons (nerve cells) do not reproduce, so if they are damaged or diseased, they cannot be replaced. In the future, nerve cells could be replaced by stem cells. Patients with Alzheimer's disease suffer a form of dementia caused by neuron loss. Stem cells could be differentiated into new neurons to replenish those lost. Stem cells could also be used to repair damage to the spinal cord, which is a major cause of paralysis.

### ▲ STEM CELLS
Once a body cell has differentiated – become a particular type such as a nerve or blood cell – it cannot turn into any other type of cell. However, stem cells are not differentiated and so have the potential to become any type of cell in the body simply by switching on and off the "correct" genes. One source of stem cells is blood (above) from a baby's umbilical cord. Scientists believe that stem cells can be used to treat diseases because they can be turned into specific cells to replace damaged tissue.

human genome

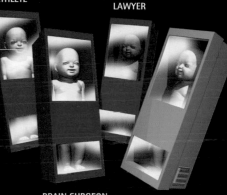

ATHLETE  LAWYER

Baby's genome modified to produce desired features

BRAIN SURGEON  ACTOR

## DNA CRIME INVESTIGATION

### SAMPLE FROM CRIME SCENE
Forensic scientists use a technique called DNA fingerprinting to help police solve crimes. Tissues such as blood, saliva, hair, or skin provide samples of their DNA. When these are found at a crime scene, they are removed carefully to avoid contamination, analysed in a forensic laboratory, and compared with the DNA of a suspect.

### DESIGNER BABIES ▶
Some diseases are caused by faulty genes being passed from parent to child. Using DNA technology, it is already possible to select fertilized eggs that do not carry the faulty gene and implant them in the uterus to produce a healthy baby. But there is concern that in the future, selection may go further – for example, scientists might attempt to add "intelligence" genes to create a designer baby that matches its parents' desires.

### DNA SAMPLE
DNA is extracted from tissue cells found at the crime scene. Samples of blood from any suspects (and the victim of the crime) are taken to provide DNA for comparison. Only small samples are needed but if only a little is available, it can be duplicated using special enzymes. The DNA sample (shown left) is then analysed.

### FUTURE IDENTITY CARD
One day we may all carry an identity card like this one. The card includes a fingerprint and iris pattern to confirm the individual's identity, together with a bar code that encodes personal information. What is different about this card is that it contains details of the person's genome, carried inside a special chip. In 20 years' time, it should be possible to sequence a person's genome cheaply and quickly. This could be completed soon after a baby is born, allowing a complete genetic profile to be added to the baby's medical record and implanted on its identity card. The DNA information could be read by doctors looking for indicators of possible future diseases. These could be corrected or avoided by a recommended change of lifestyle.

Cut is made between two bases

A A T T C

G

G

C T T A A

### ENZYMES CUTTING DNA
Each person's genome has sections of junk DNA containing base sequences that are repeated again and again. However, the lengths and numbers of repeated sections are unique to each person. This information identifies an individual as accurately as a fingerprint. Enzymes cut junk DNA (left) at specific points to produce sections of different lengths.

DNA logo indicates the card contains the genome chip

Photograph of card holder

Bar code contains personal data

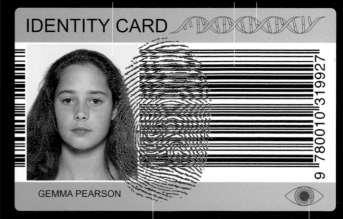

IDENTITY CARD

GEMMA PEARSON

9 780010 319927

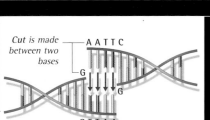

### DNA COMPARISON
The DNA sections are separated by size in a process called gel electrophoresis, which produces a pattern of bands on the gel plate called a DNA fingerprint. The DNA fingerprints from the crime scene, the suspects, and the victim, are lined up (left) to determine who committed the crime and who can be eliminated.

Fingerprint identifies the individual

Iris recognition – the iris is as individual as a fingerprint

# TIMELINE OF MEDICAL DISCOVERIES

**c.2600 BC** Chinese emperor Huang Ti lays down the basic principles of Chinese medicine, which are later recorded, in the fourth century BC, in the *Nei Ching* or *Manual of Physic*.

**c.500 BC** Greek physician Alcmaeon of Croton suggests that the brain, and not the heart, is the organ of feeling and thinking.

**c.420 BC** Greek physician Hippocrates teaches the importance of observation and diagnosis – rather than magic and myth – in medicine.

**c.200** Influential Greek-born doctor Claudius Galen describes the workings of the body. Although many of his ideas are incorrect, they remain unchallenged until the 1500s.

**c.1000** Publication by Arab doctor Ibn Sina (Avicenna) of medical texts that influence European and Middle-Eastern medicine for the next 500 years.

**c.1280** Arab physician Ibn An-Nafis demonstrates that blood flows through the lungs.

**1543** Flemish doctor Andreas Vesalius publishes the first accurate description of human anatomy in his book *On the Structure of the Human Body*, correcting many of Galen's errors.

**1545** French surgeon Ambroise Paré publishes *Methods of Treating Wounds*. His descriptions of improved techniques for treating wounds include the use of ligatures to tie arteries to stop bleeding.

**1628** English doctor William Harvey publishes *On the Movement of the Heart and Blood*, in which he describes his experiments that show how blood circulates around the body in one direction, pumped by the heart.

**1663** Italian physiologist and microscopist Marcello Malpighi discovers the smallest blood vessels, capillaries, confirming Harvey's theory that blood circulates around the body.

**1674–7** Dutch draper and microscopist Antoni van Leeuwenhoek observes and describes red blood cells, sperm, and bacteria using his single lens microscope.

**1761** Italian physician Giovanni Battista Morgagni, publishes *On the Sites and Causes of Disease* which, for the first time, describes the links between changes in organs and symptoms of disease.

**1775** French chemist Antoine Lavoisier discovers oxygen and later shows that cell respiration is, like burning, a chemical process that consumes oxygen to release energy.

**1796** British doctor Edward Jenner performs the first vaccination against the widely feared disease smallpox by inoculating a child with a vaccine containing the weaker cowpox virus.

**1816** French doctor René Théophile Hyacinthe Laënnec invents the first stethoscope – a wooden cylinder that magnifies heart and breathing sounds when pressed against the chest.

**1818** British doctor James Blundell performs the first successful transfusion of human blood to a human patient.

**1833** American army surgeon William Beaumont publishes *Experiments and Observations on the Gastric Juice and Physiology of Digestion* – the results of his experiments into the mechanisms of digestion.

**1846** American dentist William Morton uses ether and a general anaesthetic to make a patient unconscious and pain-free during an operation performed by surgeon John Warren.

**1848** French scientist Claude Bernard demonstrates the function of the liver, and later shows that body cells need to exist in stable surroundings.

**1851** German Physicist Hermann von Helmholtz invents the opthalmoscope, an instrument that allows doctors to look inside the eye through the pupil.

**1854** British doctor John Snow proves that cholera is spread by contaminated water, during an outbreak of the disease in London.

**1858** German biologist Rudolf Virchow states in his book *Cellular Pathology* that cells can only be made from existing ones through cell division, and that disease occurs when cells stop working normally.

**1860s** French scientist Louis Pasteur begins research that will prove that micro-organisms cause infectious diseases.

**1861** French doctor Pierre Paul Broca identifies an area on the left side of the brain that controls speech. This is later named Broca's area.

**1865** British surgeon Joseph Lister first uses carbolic acid as an antiseptic during surgery, dramatically reducing deaths from infection.

**1866** Clinical thermometer is developed by British physician Thomas Albutt, enabling doctors to take patients' temperatures easily and quickly.

**1867** German physician Wilhelm Waldeyer-Hartz first describes the nature and cause of cancers, describing how cells divide uncontrollably to form tumours.

**1871** German physiologist Wilhelm Kühne introduces the term "enzyme" to describe substances that activate and accelerate chemical reactions inside living organisms.

**1881** Louis Pasteur pioneers use of vaccines containing mild forms of disease-causing microbes, rather than microbes causing similar, milder diseases, to induce immunity.

**1882** German doctor Robert Koch identifies the bacterium (*Mycobacterium tuberculosis*) that causes tuberculosis (TB).

**1895** X-rays are discovered by German physicist Wilhelm Roentgen when he passes a high-voltage electric current through a glass tube.

**1897** British doctor Ronald Ross shows that the micro-organism *Plasmodium*, which causes malaria, is spread from person to person by mosquitoes.

**1898** French physicists Marie and Pierre Curie discover the radioactive element radium, later used in the treatment of cancers.

**1901** Austrian-American doctor Karl Landsteiner demonstrates the existence of blood groups – later classified as A, B, AB, and O – by showing that some blood samples clot when mixed together.

**1903** Dutch physiologist Willem Einthoven develops an early version of the electrocardiograph (ECG), a device that monitors heart activity by detecting the electrical impulses that travel through the heart during each heartbeat.

**1905** British physiologist Ernest Starling uses the term "hormone" to describe the newly-discovered chemical messengers that co-ordinate body processes by travelling in the blood to affect the activities of specific cells.

**1905** German doctor Eduard Zirm performs the first corneal transplant in the eye, enabling treatment of trachoma, a cause of blindness.

timeline

**1906** British physiologist Charles Sherrington publishes *The Integrative Action of the Nervous System*, describing how the nervous system works.

**1906-12** British biochemist Frederick Gowland Hopkins demonstrates the importance of "accessory food factors" in food. These are later called vitamins.

**1910** German scientist Paul Ehrlich discovers Salvarsan, the first drug of known composition to treat a specific pathogen without severe effects on body tissues, establishing a basis for chemotherapy.

**1912** American doctor Harvey Cushing publishes *The Pituitary Gland and its Disorder*, which describes the function of the gland and shows its importance in controlling other hormone-producing glands.

**1914** American doctor Joseph Goldberger shows that pellagra is not an infectious disease but is caused by poor diet – later shown more specifically as the lack of the vitamin niacin.

**1921** Canadian physiologists Frederick Banting and Charles Best isolate the hormone insulin, which is produced in the pancreas and controls blood glucose levels. Their discovery enables the disease diabetes to be treated.

**1921** German-born American scientist Otto Loewi detects chemicals called neurotransmitters that relay impulses between neurons at synapses.

**1924** German-born scientist Johannes Berger discovers brain waves – electrical signals produced by nervous activity inside the brain.

**1927** American bioengineers Philip Drinker and Louis Shaw develop the "iron lung" to help patients paralysed by polio. The metal tank surrounds the body (but not the head), and a pump moves air in and out of the lungs, enabling a patient to breathe.

**1928** British doctor Alexander Fleming discovers penicillin, a substance, released by a mould, that kills bacteria. It will later become the first antibiotic – a drug used to treat bacterial infections in humans.

**1933** German electrical engineer Ernst Ruska demonstrates the electron microscope – a device that uses electron beams to produce much great magnification than that achieved by light microscopes.

**1938** Hip replacement, using a stainless steel prosthesis, is developed by British surgeon John Wiles.

**1940** British surgeon Archibald McIndoe carries out the first skin grafts on World War II pilots suffering burns. Burnt areas of facial skin are replaced using skin from other areas of the body.

**1943** Dutch doctor Willem Kolff invents the kidney dialysis machine, which treats people with kidney failure by "cleaning" their blood to remove wastes and then returning it to the body.

**1943** Ukranian-American biochemist Selman Waksman isolates the antibiotic streptomycin from a soil microbe. Streptomycin is the first drug capable of treating tuberculosis (TB).

**1944** Pioneering operation to treat heart disease in a baby is carried out by American surgeon Alfred Blalock in association with paediatrician Helen Taussig. It establishes the field of cardiac surgery.

**1949** Australian psychiatrist John Cade demonstrates that the substance lithium, taken as lithium carbonate, is effective in treating mental illnesses, including schizophenia.

**1953** Using research by British physicist Rosalind Franklin, US biologist James Watson and British physicist Frances Crick discover the double helix structure of the DNA molecule.

**1953** American surgeon John Gibbon develops the heart-lung machine to take over the work of the heart and lungs during surgery.

**1954** A polio vaccine developed by American doctor Jonas Salk is used for the first time.

**1954** First successful kidney transplant, from one identical twin to another, is carried out by John Merrill and other surgeons in Boston, USA. Kidney transplants soon become routine operations.

**1955** Gregory Pincus develops the first oral contraceptive.

**1957** American surgeon Clarence Lillehei devises first compact heart pacemaker.

**1958** Ultrasound scanning first used to check the health of a fetus in its mother's uterus by British obstetrician Ian Donald.

**1961** First use of improved polio vaccine containing live virus developed by Polish-American microbiologist Albert Sabin. The vaccine can be taken by mouth, rather than being injected.

**1965** British scientist Harold Hopkins produces a sophisticated endoscope that uses rod lenses to give doctors a clear view of tissues inside the body. It is inserted through openings, such as the mouth, to view, for example, the stomach and intestines.

**1967** British engineer Godfrey Hounsfield develops the CAT scanner (now called a CT scanner). It uses narrow beams of X-rays projected through the body then analysed by computer to produce detailed images of body tissues.

**1967** South African surgeon Christiaan Barnard carries out the first successful heart transplant. He transplants the healthy heart of a 24-year-old woman who had recently died, into the body of a 54-year-old man with heart disease.

**1967** Introduction of mammography – an X-ray technique for detecting breast cancer.

**1977** Last recorded case of smallpox after a program of vaccination. The disease is declared eradicated by the World Health Organization in 1979.

**1978** The first "test tube" baby Louise Brown is born following successful in vitro fertilization (IVF) of her mother using techniques developed by British doctors Patrick Steptoe and Robert Edwards. Eggs taken from the mother's ovary are fertilized using the father's sperm and returned to the uterus to develop into a baby.

**1980** Introduction of "keyhole" surgery using small incisions and an endoscope to look inside the body.

**1980s** PET scans first used to produce images of brain activity.

**1984** French scientist Luc Montagnier discovers the virus – later called human immunodeficiency virus (HIV) – that causes acquired immunodeficiency syndrome (AIDS). AIDS was first identified in 1981.

**2000** First "draft" of Human Genome Project – an international research project to map the genes in human chromosomes – is completed.

**2002** Gene therapy used to cure boys suffering from an inherited immunodeficiency disease that leaves the body defenceless against infection.

**2003** Following encouraging trials using monkeys, Belgian doctors begin to test an experimental HIV/AIDS vaccine on humans to determine its effectiveness in preventing infection with HIV.

# GLOSSARY

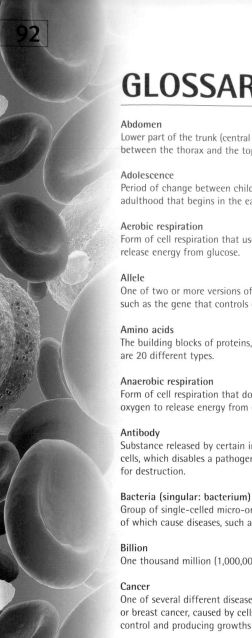

**Abdomen**
Lower part of the trunk (central part of the body) between the thorax and the top of the legs.

**Adolescence**
Period of change between childhood and adulthood that begins in the early teen years.

**Aerobic respiration**
Form of cell respiration that uses oxygen to release energy from glucose.

**Allele**
One of two or more versions of the same gene, such as the gene that controls eye colour.

**Amino acids**
The building blocks of proteins, of which there are 20 different types.

**Anaerobic respiration**
Form of cell respiration that does not require oxygen to release energy from glucose.

**Antibody**
Substance released by certain immune system cells, which disables a pathogen and marks it for destruction.

**Bacteria (singular: bacterium)**
Group of single-celled micro-organisms, some of which cause diseases, such as TB, in humans.

**Billion**
One thousand million (1,000,000,000).

**Cancer**
One of several different diseases, such as lung or breast cancer, caused by cells dividing out of control and producing growths called tumours.

**Carbon dioxide**
Gas that is the waste product of cell respiration and is expelled from the body by breathing out.

**Cardiac**
Describes something related to the heart.

**Cartilage**
Tough connective tissue that covers the ends of bones in joints and helps to support the body.

**Cell respiration**
The release of energy from glucose and other fuels, which takes place in the cytoplasm and mitochondria of cells.

**Chemoreceptor**
Sensory receptor, such as those in the tongue, that detects chemicals dissolved in water.

**Cilia (singular: cilium)**
Tiny, hair-like projections from certain body cells that beat to move objects and substances, such as mucus, across their surface.

**Computed tomography (CT) scan**
Imaging technique that uses X-rays and computers to produce "slices" through, and 3-D images of, living tissues.

**Connective tissue**
A tissue such as cartilage that holds together other tissues and supports the body.

**Consciousness**
Awareness of self and surroundings produced by areas of the brain's cerebral cortex.

**Coronary heart disease**
The narrowing of coronary arteries that supply the heart wall with blood, causing damage to the cardiac muscle.

**Diagnosis**
Identification by a doctor of a disorder or disease using signs and symptoms described by the patient.

**Diaphragm**
Dome-shaped sheet of muscle that separates the thorax from the abdomen and plays an important part in breathing.

**Disease**
A failure in one or more of the body's control systems, usually short-lived and corrected by the body itself.

**DNA (Deoxyribonucleic acid)**
Molecules found inside body cells that consist of two intertwined nucleic acid strands that carry the genetic instructions needed to build and operate that cell.

**Electrocardiogram (ECG)**
Recording made by an electrocardiograph of the electrical changes that occur as the heart beats.

**Electroencephalogram (EEG)**
Recording made by an electroencephalograph of brain waves produced by electrical activity in the brain.

**Electron microscope**
Microscope that uses a beam of electrons focused by magnets to produced highly magnified images of body tissue.

**Embryo**
Name given to a developing baby in the first eight weeks following fertilization.

**Endoscope**
Flexible viewing instrument used for looking inside the body's hollow organs and cavities.

**Energy**
The capacity to perform work, essential to keep cells functioning.

**Enzyme**
Protein catalyst that greatly accelerates the rate of chemical reactions inside and outside cells and plays a key role in digestion.

**Fetus**
Name given to a baby developing in the uterus from the ninth week after fertilization to birth.

**Fibrocartilage**
Type of cartilage, rich in collagen, found in the discs between vertebrae.

**Gastric**
Describes something relating to the stomach.

**Gel electrophoresis**
Technique used to separate molecules of different size by applying an electric current across a gel column, which carries the molecules.

**Genetic code**
Code used to convert the instructions carried by the sequence of bases in DNA into a sequence of amino acids in a protein.

**Genome**
The DNA contained in a set of chromosomes; in humans there are 23 chromosomes.

**Gland**
Collection of cells that secretes a chemical substance into or on the body.

**Gut**
Alternative name for the alimentary canal.

**Hepatic**
Describes something relating to the liver.

**Hormone**
Chemical "message" that is made and released by an endocrine (hormone-producing) gland to affect the activity of target cells.

**Hyaline cartilage**
Type of cartilage, shiny in appearance, that covers bone ends in joints.

**Hypothalamus**
Part of the brain that regulates body temperature, hunger, thirst, and other body activities through the nervous system or, via the pituitary gland, through the endocrine system.

**Infection**
Growth of disease-causing micro-organisms, such as bacteria, either on or inside the body.

**Karyotype**
Photograph of a complete set of chromosomes organized in order of size.

**Ligament**
Strips of tough, fibrous connective tissue that hold bones together where they meet at joints.

**Light microscope**
Instrument that uses light focused by glass lenses to produce a magnified image.

**Magnetic resonance angiography (MRA)**
MRI used to produce images of blood vessels.

**Magnetic resonance imaging (MRI)**
Imaging technique that uses magnetism, radio waves, and a computer to produce images of soft and hard tissues inside the body.

**Magnetoencephalography (MEG)**
Imaging technique that produces images of brain activity.

**Mechanoreceptor**
Sensory receptor, such as those found in the skin and ear, that detects pressure produced by touch or sound waves.

**Melanin**
Pigment that colours the skin, hair, and eyes.

**Messenger RNA (mRNA)**
Molecule that copies sections of DNA and carries the "message" from the nucleus to be translated into protein structure in the cytoplasm.

**Metabolism**
Sum total of all the chemical reactions that take place inside body cells.

**Microbe**
Common name for a micro-organism.

**Micrograph**
Photograph taken with the aid of a light or electron microscope.

**Micro-organism**
Living thing, such as a bacterium, that can only be seen by using a microscope.

**Millisecond (msec)**
One thousandth of a second (0.001 sec).

**Mitosis**
The separation of the chromosomes that takes place when cell division produces two identical cells from each "parent" cell.

**Mitochondria (singular: mitochondrion)**
Cell organelles inside which aerobic respiration takes place to release energy.

**Mucus**
Thick, slimy fluid produced by the respiratory and digestive systems to protect and lubricate.

**Nanotechnology**
Technology that utilizes microscopic components.

**Negative feedback**
Control mechanism inside the body that reverses an unwanted change, such as an increase in body temperature or excessive amounts of a hormone in the blood.

**Nerve impulse**
"Message" in the form of a electrical signal that travels along a nerve fibre at high speed.

**Neurotransmitter**
Chemical released when a nerve impulse reaches the end of a nerve fibre at a synapse, triggering a nerve impulse in a neighbouring neuron.

**Nitrogenous base**
One of four bases (adenine, cytosine, guanine, and thymine) that create "messages" carried by DNA.

**Nociceptor**
Sensory receptor that responds to potentially damaging stimuli, resulting in pain.

**Nutrient**
Food substances, such as carbohydrate, needed in the diet for normal body functioning.

**Organ**
Body part, such as the stomach, that has one or more specific roles, and is made up of two or more types of tissue.

**Organelle**
Structure inside a cell, such as a mitochondrion, that has a specific function or functions.

**Ossification**
The process through which bone is produced.

**Oxygen**
Gas that is taken into the body during breathing in and used by cells to release energy from glucose during cell respiration.

**Pathogen**
Bacterium, virus, protist, fungus, or any other micro-organism that causes disease in humans.

**Phagocyte**
Common name for white blood cells (including neutrophils and macrophages), which engulf and destroy invading pathogens.

**Photoreceptor**
Receptor in the eye that detects light.

**Placenta**
Organ that develops in the uterus during pregnancy to provide the fetus with food and oxygen and remove its wastes.

**Positron emission topography (PET)**
Imaging technique that uses radioactive substances injected into the body to reveal activity in the brain and some organs.

**Pregnancy**
The period between an embryo implanting the in the uterus and the birth of the fully developed baby, usually 38–40 weeks.

**Protein**
One of a group of substances inside the body that perform many roles including building cells, carrying oxygen, and making enzymes.

**Protist**
Member of a group of single-celled micro-organisms, some of which cause diseases, such as malaria, in humans.

**Radioactive**
Describes a substance that gives off atomic particles that may be harmful to humans.

**Radionuclide scan**
Imaging technique that uses radioactive substances to reveal activity in bones and some other tissues.

**Radiotherapy**
Use of high-energy radiation to kill cancer cells.

**Receptor**
Sensory cell that responds to a stimulus such as light or touch by generating a nerve impulse that travels along a neuron.

**Reflex action**
Automatic, unchanging, unconscious, and rapid response to a stimulus, which, in some instances, protects the body from danger.

**Renaissance**
Period between the 14th and 16th centuries in Europe when there was a surge of interest in the arts and sciences.

**Synapse**
Junction between neighbouring neurons in where they are separated by a small gap.

**Surgery**
Direct treatment of a disease or injury, often by opening the body using surgical instruments.

**Thermography**
Imaging technique that uses heat released by the body to produce a colour-coded image.

**Thorax**
The upper part of the trunk (the central part of the body) between the abdomen and the neck.

**Tissue**
Collection of one type, or similar types, of cell that work together to carry out a particular function.

**Trillion**
One million million (1,000,000,000,000).

**Tumour**
Abnormal growth of tissue caused by the division of cells at an increased rate.

**Ultrasound**
Imaging technique that uses high-frequency sound waves to produce images of the growing fetus, and other body tissues.

**Ultraviolet (UV) radiation**
Radiation that occurs naturally in sunlight, which can be harmful to skin in cases of over-exposure.

**Urogram**
X-ray photograph of the urinary system produced by introducing a contrast medium into the system.

**Virus**
Non-living agent that causes diseases such as measles and colds in humans.

**X-ray**
Type of high-energy radiation that reveals bones when projected through the body onto photographic film.

**Zygote**
Cell produced when a sperm fertilizes an egg.

# INDEX

# ACKNOWLEDGEMENTS

**Dorling Kindersley** would like to thank Lynn Bresler for proof-reading and for the index; Margaret Parrish for Americanization; and Tony Cutting for DTP support.

Dorling Kindersley Ltd is not responsible and does not accept liability for the availability or content of any website other than its own, or for any exposure to offensive, harmful, or inaccurate material that may appear on the Internet. Dorling Kindersley Ltd will have no liability for any damage or loss caused by viruses that may be downloaded as a result of looking at and browsing the website that it recommends. Dorling Kindersley downloadable images are the sole copyright of Dorling Kindersley Ltd, and may not be reproduced, stored, or transmitted in any form or by any means for any commercial or profit-related purpose without prior written permission of the copyright owner.

**Picture Credits**

The publisher would like to thank the following for their kind permission to reproduce their photographs:

**Abbreviations key:**
a=above; b=bottom/below; c=centre; l=left; r=right; t=top

4-5 Science Photo Library: D.Phillips. 8 akg-images: (bl).; The Art Archive: Dagli Orti (tl); Science Photo Library: (cr), (br); The Wellcome Institute Library, London: (c). 9 Science Photo Library: Christian Darkin (r), Du Cane Medical Imaging Ltd. (cb), Mehau Kulyk (ca), Montreal Neurological Institute (c), PH. Saada/Eurelios (c), Simon Fraser (l), VVG (bc), Zephyr (cbb). 10 DK Images: Geoff Dann/Donkin Models (b); Science Photo Library: Eric Grave (tr). 11 Science Photo Library: David McCarthy (cr), Michael Abbey (tc), (tr), (tcr), Prof. P. Motta/Dept. of Anatomy/University, "La Sapienza", Rome (tl), VVG (br). 12 Science Photo Library: Innerspace Imaging (c), VVG (tc), (ca). 13 Science Photo Library: Alfred Pasieka (tc), Biophoto Associates (tcr), Profs. P.M. Motta,

K.R. Porter & P.M. Andrews (tr). 14 Getty Images (tr); Science Photo Library: Innerspace Imaging (bl), Institut Paoli-Calmettes, ISM (br). 15 Science Photo Library: Michael Donne, University of Manchester (bl), (br), (bcl), (bcr), Susan Leavines (tl). 16 Science Photo Library: David Scharf (tr), Prof. P. Motta/ Dept. Of Anatomy, University "La Sapienza", Rome (bc), (tcr), WG (cbl). 17 NASA: (tr); Science Photo Library: (bl), (bcl), Andrew Syred (tl). 19 Science Photo Library: David Mooney (tcr), Du Cane Medical Imaging Ltd. (cr), Mike Devlin (cla), Sam Ogden (tr), Zephyr (c). 20 Science Photo Library: (bc), (bcr), Biophoto Associates (br). 21 Corbis: Roininen Juha/ Sygma (tr), Corbis Royalty Free (cr). 22 Science Photo Library: David Becker (tr). 23 Science Photo Library: Don Fawcett (tl), VVG (bl). 24 Science Photo Library: P. Hattenberger, Publiphoto Diffusion (cl), Tony McConnell (bl); 24-25 Getty Images: Art Montes De Oca. 25 The Wellcome Institute Library, London: (cla), (ca), (ca2). 26 Science Photo Library: David Becker (tl), Susumu Nishinaga (ca). 27 Science Photo Library: Andrew Syred (crbb) CNRI (crb), Eye of Science (c), (br), J.C. Revy (tr), VVG (tl). 28 Science Photo Library: Dr. P. Marazzi (bc), Sheila Terry (bl). 29 Science Photo Library: CNRI (bc), J.C. Revy (c), Lawrence Lawry (tr). 30 Science Photo Library: Adam Hart-Davis (clb), (bl). 31 Science Photo Library: Geoff Bryant (br poppy backgrounds), VVG (cr). 32 Science Photo Library: CNRI (ca), (cl), Susumu Nishinga (br). 33 Science Photo Library: John Bavosi (br). 34 Science Photo Library: CNRI (bl). 35 Alamy Images: David Sanger (tl); 35 Science Photo Library: Omikron (bl). 38 Science Photo Library: Zephyr (bl). 40 Photovault: (b); Science Photo Library: CNRI (tr). 41 Photovault: (t); Science Photo Library: Hank Morgan (cr), Oscar Burriel (br), Zephyr (cl), (cb). 42 Getty Images: Vera Storman (cl), (bc). 43 Corbis: Charles Gupton (tcr), Rick Gomez (tr); Getty Images: (c); Science Photo Library: Mark Lewis (tc). 45 Corbis: Nik Wheeler (bl). 47 Science Photo Library: VVG (cb), Zephyr (bl). 48 Science Photo Library: (cb), Philippe Plailly (br). 49 Science Photo Library: BSIP, Joubert (br) Scott Camazine (bc). 52 Science Photo Library:

(craa), Biophoto Associates (cl), Dr.Linda Stannard, UCT (cra), Eye of Science (tr), John Durham (br), Prof. P. Motta/Dept of Anatomy/University, "La Sapienza" Rome (crbb), Profs. P.M. Motta, K.R. Porter & P.M. Andrews (bl), Profs. P.M.Motta, K.R. Porter & P.M. Andrews (bl), VVG (clb). 53 Alamy Images: (br); Science Photo Library: Eye of Science (t); VVG (cl). 55 Science Photo Library: Ian Boddy (bl), NIBSC (tr). 56 Corbis: David Michael Zimmerman (crb), Science Photo Library: Simon Fraser/ Royal Victoria Infirmary, Newcastle Upon Tyne (bc). 56-57 Corbis: Lester Lefkowitz (t). 57 Science Photo Library: AJ Photo/Hop Americain (br), BSIP, Raguet (tr), Mauro Fermariello (clb), Pascal Goetgeluck (bl), SIU (cl), Will & Deni McIntyre (clbb). 59 Corbis: Reuters (tl); Science Photo Library: David M. Martin, M.D. (tc), (cl), (bl). 61 Science Photo Library: (bc), Alex Bartel (br), BSIP VEM (tr), Dr. Tony Brain (bl), Susumu Nishinaga (cr). 62 Science Photo Library: Dr. K.F.R. Schiller (bl), Eye of Science (crb), Prof. P. Motta & F. Magliocca/University "La Sapienza", Rome (br), Prof. P. Motta/ Dept. of Anatomy/University "La Sapienza", Rome (cr), (tr), VVG (cra). 63 Science Photo Library: David Scharf (bl) Scimat (cr). 65 Digital Vision: (bl). 66 Science Photo Library: CNRI (bl), Pascal Goetgeluck (cl). 67 Science Photo Library: Alfred Pasieka (tr), Dr. Arnold Brody (cb), Hossler, Custom Medical Stock Photo (cl), James Steveson (bc), (cbb). 69 Corbis: Jeffrey L. Rotman (cr); Science Photo Library: Biophoto Associates (tc). 70 Science Photo Library: CNRI (bl), (br). 71 Alamy Images: Jacky Chapman (tl); Pa Photos: Phil Noble (cl); 71 Science Photo Library: Wellcome Dept. of Cognitive Neurology (br), (crb), (br). 72 Science Photo Library: Prof. P. Motta/Dept. of Anatomy/University "La Sapienza", Rome (bc), Professor P. Motta & D. Palermo (tc). 73 Science Photo Library: Adam Hart-Davis (bl), (bcl), CNRI (cl), Dr. Gopal Murti (cr), Prof. P. Motta/Dept. of Anatomy/University "La Sapienza", Rome (ccl), VVG (ccr). 74 Science Photo Library: VVG (crb). 75 Science Photo Library: (clb), (bl). 76 Science Photo Library: CNRI (crb), (bc). 77 Science Photo Library: Prof. P. Motta/Dept. of

Anantomy/University "La Sapienza", Rome (cb), Professors P.M. Motta, G. Macchiarelli, S.A. Nottola (cr). 78 Science Photo Library: D. Phillips (l), Dr O. Moscoso bcl, Professor R. Motta, Department of Anatomy, Rome University (crb), Professors P.M. Motta & J. Van Blerkom (cra); The Wellcome Institute Library, London: Yorgos Nikas (bcr). 79 LOGIQlibrary: (tl), (tc), (tr); Getty Images: Ranald Mackechnie (bl); Science Photo Library: Du Cane Medical Imaging Ltd (cl); The Wellcome Institute Library, London: Anthea Sieveking (br). 80 Science Photo Library: (bl). 80-81 Getty Images: Photodisc Collection (c). 81 Alamy Images: David young-Wolff (cb); Corbis: Ariel Skelley (br); Science Photo Library: (tr). 82 Getty Images: Ryan McVey (cl); Science Photo Library: Andrew Syred (bcr), Dr. P. Marazzi (bcl), Scott Camazine (bl). 83 Corbis: Jim Richardson (cr), Tom Stewart (tl); Science Photo Library: (bc), Alfred Pasieka (br), Zephyr (bl). 84 DK Images: Geoff Dann / Donkin Models (tl); Science Photo Library: Andrew Syred (c). 85 Science Photo Library: CNRI (tl), Lauren Shear (tr). 86 Science Photo Library: Alfred Pasieka (cb), (t), Innerspace Imaging (br), Kenneth Eward/Biografx (cl), VVG (clb). 87 Corbis: George Shelley (cr); Getty Images: Barros & Barros (tl); Science Photo Library: Eye of Science (br). 88 Science Photo Library: James King-Holmes (br), Pilippe Plailly (tl). 89 Science Photo Library: Colin Cuthbert (tl), Mauro Fermariello (cla), (bl), Philippe Plailly (cl) Victor Habbick Visions (cra), VVG (tr).

**Jacket images**

**Front:** Science Photo Library: Alfred Pasieka (cl), (r;), BSIP Estiot (l), National Cancer Institute (cr). **Spine:** Science Photo Library: National Cancer Institute. **Back:** Corbis: Douglas Kirkland (l); Science Photo Library: Astrid & Hanns-Frieder Michler (cl), Bernard Benoit (r), VVG (cr).

All other images © Dorling Kindersley. For further information see: **www.dkimages.com**